John N. Cole

Books

    In Maine
    From the Ground Up (with Charles Wing)
    Striper: A Story of Fish and Man
    Amaranth
    Cityside/Countryside
    Sun Reflections: Images for a Solar Age
    Salmon
    Breaking New Ground (with Charles Wing)
    Fishing Came First
    Tarpon Quest
    Away All Boats
    Fish of My Years
    West of Key West

Anthologies

    Coast Alert
    Wonders
    Crossroads: Environmental Priorities for the Future
    Boats
    Fathers & Sons
    The Seaside Reader

*Life*List

Life List

Remembering the Birds of My Years

John N. Cole

Illustrations by Marvin Kuhn

Down East Books

5   4   3   2   1

Down East Books / Camden, Maine

Library of Congress Cataloging-in-Publication Data

Cole, John N., 1923-
    Life list : remembering the birds of my years / by John N. Cole.
        p.   cm.
    ISBN 0-89272-415-3 (hardcover)
    1. Birds—Anecdotes. 2. Bird watching—Anecdotes. 3. Cole, John
N., 1923-   . I. Title.
    QL 795.B57C58   1997
    598'.07'234—dc21
                                                        97-26445
                                                          CIP

For Chick

Acknowledgments

For his superb illustrations, all of us must thank Marvin Kuhn— artist, bird-watcher, and gentle man—who has maintained a lifelong awareness of the world around him. Many of these portraits have appeared in *The East Hampton Star*, one of the nation's oldest and finest weekly newspapers. My thanks to the *Star* for allowing us to share Marvin's artistry.

Contents

Life list—A bird-watcher's record, usually organized by species, of his or her confirmed bird sightings over the years. Some life lists include hundreds of birds.

Prologue

My first steps each morning are toward the window. It's a compulsion. I want to study the sky, be reassured that the natural world is still out there. I do it, I suppose, the way some folks say their daily prayers.

I've been doing it ever since I can remember, and that's quite a few decades now. No matter where I travel in the world, no matter which house or office I enter for the first time, I move toward the windows. And when we had that once-in-a-lifetime chance to design and build our own new home, its entire, long southeast side was glass, from floor to roof.

When we sited the house, I stood on top of a wheelbarrow and declared that spot would be our bedroom and decreed that corner would locate each of the others because from there I had the finest view of the woods and water that spilled toward the open ocean eight miles south. In that house, when I awakened, windows were there waiting.

Looking back now, recognizing (but not comprehending) this compulsion, I can understand how I met so many birds. After all, birds are the majority tenants of the visible outdoors. They step along lawns, fly from tree to tree, sweep across the skies in great undulating flocks, pick their way daintily along the water's edge, glide down dark clouds, dive from unseen heights above, and call to you as their shadows sweep along the edge of your awareness.

It's taken me most of a lifetime to establish a working relationship with birds. I no longer shoot at any of them. Yet I will not deny the excitement of my bird-hunting years. They happened, and they brought me some of the finest memories of those years.

On one of those hunts I met a man who spent his entire life and career caring for the game birds on the vast plantation he supervised. It was his job to make certain that visiting hunters found game in abundance.

When he and I met, he had at least thirty gunning seasons and hundreds of gunners to review. "I've watched them grow up and seen some of them grow old," he said to me. "And I've learned there are two kinds of hunters. Some of them become better and better shots. That's their goal: to see how many birds they can shoot in a day. Then there are the hunters who shoot less and less as the years pass. Soon they quit altogether. They just put away their guns."

It took more than thirty years for me to put away my guns, and when I did I remembered what that wise man had said. I had become one of the hunters who would kill no more birds, although when he spoke with me I was certain I would become one of those who never quit trying to be a better shot. We know ourselves, I suppose, least of all.

One thing I do know: I can't imagine my life without birds. Like our children, like my home landscape, like each of the people I love and have loved, the birds have always been there, natural icons marking each passage and experience. They have put their names on the years, the places, the adventures and misadventures, the pleasures, and the miseries of the days and nights under the sky, out there beyond the windows where the wind slaps your face and snow crunches under your boots.

This is the story of some of those birds that have left their marks on my life.

NORTHERN
SAW-WHET OWL
(Aegolius acadius)

Two years after I began a city career in a Manhattan office, I left to become a commercial fisherman on Long Island's east end. I quit in October—not a smart move. Except for offshore codfishing from a dory out there on the freezing Atlantic, there was not much winter fishing off Long Island unless you worked aboard one of the few draggers that trawled the stormy seas.

So Jim and I cut firewood and painted houses to earn money while we waited for spring. And while we painted, we dreamed and talked about fishing. But when we cut firewood, we tried to pay attention to our work— especially after the morning I dropped a medium-large white oak onto my Model A Ford.

That tree caved in the driver's-side roof and shattered the window. Jim was too disgusted with his new firewood partner to help me repair the damage, and I wasn't sure how. I spent the rest of that winter driving a mostly open car. I kept a knitted watch cap pulled down to my eyebrows and a scarf wrapped up over my nose.

That's how I was dressed one snowy night as I drove along East Hampton's Dunmere Lane. The snowflakes were big fat ones, swirling like white moths in the glow of the Model A's under-powered headlights. I couldn't see more than ten feet ahead, but I knew the road well and chugged along about twenty miles an hour.

The road was silent under the soft snow, and every landmark had vanished. I seemed to be flying.

I saw a bird, or thought I did, in the headlights. Only for a flickering moment. Then I heard a soft thump, as if a small snowball had hit the fender.

I pulled over, stopped the car, and stepped out into the snow. When my eyes adjusted, I could see a small dark shape back there, between my tire tracks. I walked back and looked closely. It was a bird, lying very still. I picked it up, warm in my bare hand. I could feel its heart beating.

"Just knocked it cold," I told myself as I went back to the Model A and stuck my hand in front of a headlight. The bird was an owl: it had the round head and distinctive, stubby owl shape. But it was smaller than any owl I had ever seen or even knew about. It was soft, rufous brown touched with dark orange. White streaks dappled its breast, and quizzical white eyebrows gave its face a "What's happening?" look.

I wanted it to live and I wanted to know what sort of tiny owl it could be. With the bird in my lap, I did a one-eighty in the snow and headed back the way I had come, to the one place I knew my questions would be answered: Doc Helmuth's house on Ocean Avenue, about a mile away.

Doctor William Helmuth was indeed an M.D. who practiced in a New York City hospital. I never asked, but I assumed he worked an irregular schedule because he spent most of his time in East Hampton, and most of that time outdoors. He was one of the country's pioneer birders, an amateur ornithologist who knew as much as many of the scientists. He was a friend of Roger Tory Peterson and had been birding with the *Field Guide* author many times.

But even better, Doc Helmuth was one of the few adults that our parents told us to stay away from. That's because he was one of the only grown-ups that my two brothers and I ever did spend much time with. The other reasons, I suppose, were his reputation as an eccentric and his somewhat left-of-center politics. He was tall and gangly, had white, wispy hair, and apparently stayed up all night and slept very little during the day. Always smiling and hospitable, he made us feel welcome in his home whenever we arrived, and he spent a good deal of time teaching my youngest brother, Roddy, seven years my junior, to be a serious birder.

We were at Georgica Pond when I first decided he was a man worth knowing. Doc Helmuth's brother-in-law George Scott (the men had both married Keck sisters from California) lived in the outermost house on the dunes, and Will Helmuth spent considerable time there. The pond's flats and the narrow strip of beach that separated Georgica from the Atlantic was a splendid spot for shorebirds, a truly wild place just a few miles from the village. Peter Scott and his brothers, Henry and Tommy, were our good friends and the reason why I was at Georgica the day Will Helmuth ate the silversides.

These small fish, also called spearing, are translucent, with pale see-through flesh and a brilliant silver strip running from their black eyes to their tail. They were everywhere in Georgica, and that day a school quivered and twitched in about two inches of water over the white sands of the ocean beach. Doc Helmuth, who was waiting for a flock of shorebirds to settle, suddenly swept a long arm down and across the water's surface, with his cupped hand extended. After the explosive splash had dwindled, a half-dozen silversides flipped like twinkling coins, high and dry on the beach. Doc picked up one and bit it in half, chewing on the fragile flesh.

"Umm, delicious," he said after he'd swallowed. "Nothing better. Here, want a taste?" And he held out another wriggling minnow.

I told him no thanks. But it was a memorable moment, especially for a teenager who had never heard of sushi.

A few tumultuous years (including World War II) had passed since that day, but Will Helmuth looked much the same when I knocked at his door on that snowy night. And he was just as friendly.

I held the owl out in my hand. " I hit it with the car," I said, "But it's still alive."

"That's a little saw-whet," he said. "Aren't they beautiful? Must have gotten a bump on the head." He put his hand gently on the small, tawny breast with its white stripes. "Good strong heartbeat," he said, "and regular respiration. He may recover. I'll get something to put him in, let him lie down." He left and came back soon with a shoe box and a soft cloth folded in the bottom. He put the owl in, lying down on its back. I could see its tiny chest rising and falling as it breathed.

"It's good and warm in here," Doc Helmuth said. "I don't think there's anything we can do except wait. How did you find him?"

I told him, and he said, "Yes, they often hunt by roads. They are great little hunters. They watch for field mice and voles crossing the road. Saw-whets work hard all night and sleep all day. I've found them roosting in the thick woods and picked them up, they were sleeping so soundly. But I've never had one in the house before."

A few minutes later we stopped chatting when both of us heard a soft rustle in the box. When we peered in, the saw-whet's eyes were open and one of his clawed talons scraped against the side of the box as he sought the purchase that might allow him to get to his feet. Doc Helmuth reached in and gently stood the small bird upright.

I had to laugh. That owl rocked and blinked its wide, yellow and black eyes like a boxer coming around after being down for the count. If it could have spoken, that bewildered saw-whet would have asked, "Where am I?"

As the minutes passed, our patient's full recovery appeared to be well on the way. His rocking stopped and he began to turn his head the way owls do: almost completely around, so he could get a full, 360-degree look at his surroundings. He took it all in with a fine equanimity as if this weren't the first time he'd been in someone's sitting room. He was so unperturbed and curious that I found myself thinking of him as a small person, and a charming one at that. I was very grateful for his recovery. How terrible it would have been, I thought, if this whimsical, tiny owl had died in that collision with my Model A.

Doc Helmuth warmed some milk on the stove, added a drop

of brandy, and used an eye-dropper to feed the saw-whet a bit of the formula. When the dropper's tip touched the owl's hooked beak, the bird opened his mouth and Doc Helmuth squeezed the dropper's bulb once he got the tip well inside. We could see the saw-whet's throat working as he swallowed.

After a half-hour, Doc lifted the owl from the box and put him on the mantel above the fireplace, where he stood as imposingly as Poe's raven perched in the poet's library. With his wide eyes blinking every now and then in the light and his round head turning from side to side, that saw-whet added an unexpected and feral presence that altered the room's entire character. It was a captivating and unforgettable scene: a meeting of man and nature that I never would have believed possible until that snowy night.

"I think he'll be OK, don't you?" Doc Helmuth said. "Come back tomorrow if you want."

"You mean he's going to stay where he is? He won't fly into a wall or try to get away?"

"No, I don't think so. I'll leave the light on, and he won't go too far. He'll think it's daytime and take a snooze. Probably be the best thing for him."

When I dropped by the next afternoon, Doc Helmuth's blue eyes sparkled. "Come along," he said. "You'll like this."

As soon as I walked into the sitting room, I looked right into the eyes of that tiny owl, still perched on the mantel but commanding it now, his head turning quickly, his eyes bright and intent as they tracked every motion, every presence. A small streak of white droppings on the paneling told me the bird's systems were functioning as intended. Doc Helmuth, I thought to myself, is about the only person I know who doesn't pay any attention to an owl's crapping on his mantel.

"Now watch," he said as he reached into a small bowl on the coffee table and took out a pinch of ground beef. He shaped it into a tiny hamburger a bit smaller than a golf ball and waved it back and forth a few times under the owl's nose. Then he rolled the meatball across the sitting room floor.

Without a sound, the saw-whet left his perch, swooped down

on silent wings, snatched up the morsel in his talons, and flew back to his perch. There he held the mini-burger between his feet and began yanking off shreds with his curved beak. In a few minutes the meat was gone and the saw-whet's head was whipping around as he scanned the room for his next helping.

"I'd say he's made a full recovery, wouldn't you?" Doc Helmuth said. "I'm going to try to get a couple of snapshots and then I'll let him go."

I knew that was the right thing to do, but I wished I could keep that owl as my pet. Impossible, of course. But there was something about sharing space with a wild bird of prey that captivated me. And for the first time I realized that killing birds with a shotgun was a limited way of getting to know them. Which didn't mean I was going to quit bird hunting then and there. But the first doubts were planted by that small saw-whet.

"Your brother Roddy is getting to be quite a birder," Doc Helmuth said as I was leaving. "You should come along the next time he and I go out. You know, I could probably show you where to find owls like this one roosting back in the thick pines. You can reach out and touch them sometimes. They aren't afraid.

"Here. Here's a book for you. It's an old Chapman. I've got another. If you run into any more birds, you'll be able to tell what kind they are."

That *Handbook of Birds* by ornithologist Frank M. Chapman was first published in 1895 and revised in 1912. Now it's a hundred years old and I still have it. Unlike some later bird guides, this one has a substantial text written for ornithology students. I didn't read much of that text during the years just after Doc gave me the book, but I did later in life and I learned a great deal.

But not as much as I learned watching Doc Helmuth and that saw-whet when they first met.

Black-bellied Plover
(Pluvialis squatarola)

Surely during the summer of 1941 I should have been aware that there was a war going on, yet I have no memory of concern or apprehension. Prep school was behind me; my freshman year at Yale lay on the September horizon. I was there between the two, so naively unaware, so determinedly carefree that I could have been on another planet, a summer world where only bright days dawned on sunlit adventures unfolding one after the other like pages turned in a book of rainbows.

I had one job, one daily responsibility for which I was paid. But it was not a job that anyone called work, especially not I. Each morning and evening I would exercise a pointer named Joe for my friend Wyman Aldrich.

I was never sure why Wyman needed a bird-hunting dog, especially one as witless and high-strung as Joe: a gray, white and liver pointer trimmed lean by his constant activity. A bit less than a year old when I met him, that dog had about torn Wyman's modest home to pieces. I could see why Mrs. Aldrich had ordered him out. Wyman built a kennel in the backyard and fenced-in a cramped run. Which just about drove Joe over the brink. He howled day and night, dug huge escape holes under the fenced run, and all but stopped eating.

That's when Wyman gave me the job of taking Joe out for a run every morning and evening. The Aldrich place was less than a mile

from the Maidstone Club's golf course, built alongside the Atlantic Ocean and around Hook Pond. Brackish and about two miles long, the pond was bordered by cattails and dotted here and there with mud flats—the ideal habitat for most of the shorebirds that spent their summers on Long Island's east end. There were no golfers on the course much before nine in the morning, and by seven on those long summer evenings they had about finished their matches. But early in the morning and just before sunset, great flocks of birds gathered along the Hook Pond flats and on the golf course fairways and putting greens.

And it was in the early morning and evening when Joe took me on his runs. If that dog had been a human being he would not have been allowed out. He would have spent his days in a padded cell; he was nuts, just plain nuts. I'd let him off his leash when we got to the fourth hole across the bridge over the pond, on the part of the course that bordered the ocean.

I tried a few commands, like "heel" and "here Joe," but they never worked. That dog just ran. And fast. And far. He ran in circles, he ran straight ahead, he ran behind me and around me. He ran into the pond and out, across the black mud flats and back, into the sand traps, and along the fairways, his nose close to the ground as if he knew what he was doing.

But he didn't have a clue. And whenever he saw a flock of shorebirds, he'd head straight for them, barreling along in great loping strides that carried him headlong into the flock's nervous center. Then the birds would take wing together, calling to each other. The flocks would turn in unison so the sun caught their wings, then their breasts, light and dark against the sky, whirling and banking with a kind of graceful airborne precision that I had never before seen. When they would alight, all of them together, a half a mile across the fairways, Joe would gather his loose, lanky legs under him and go galloping off, listening only to his own demented compulsions.

I would have to run to catch him when, at last, he paused to nose some interesting mystery the birds had left behind: the scent of the wild. I'd snap the long clothesline leash to his collar and we'd start the walk back to Wyman's with Joe's muzzle pale with foam and his nervous restlessness still at full strength.

One early September evening when I returned a wriggling and drooling Joe to his pen, I asked Wyman, with appropriate indifference, what he hoped to do with what I believed was a useless creature.

"Oh," he said, "there are still a few quail in Florida. I'm kind of hoping Joe will learn how to find one or two. I don't have to travel too far down there to get some pretty fair shooting."

If I'd been a bettor, I would have wagered a fortune that Joe would never learn to execute the simplest command or acquire the intelligence to outwit a quail. But I kept quiet.

That mention of hunting seemed to stimulate Wyman's bird-shooting energies. After all, it was September; the crisp promise of fall put an edge on the air. For whatever reason, he impulsively decided to relive his early days as a shorebird gunner and he invited me along.

Those memories of his went back to the first two decades of the twentieth century—when Wyman was in his twenties and thirties. Then plover, whimbrels, curlews, godwits, turnstones, and more could be taken, spring and fall, by gunners who built blinds on the flats and marshes and set out shorebird decoys. Audubon tells us of a flight of "millions" of golden plover near New Orleans on a day when some forty-eight thousand were killed between sunrise and sunset.

Similar excess continued through the late nineteenth century until, one by one, almost all shorebirds were protected by federal law. Including the black-bellied plover. But you never would have guessed it if you had seen Wyman climbing the steps from his cellar with an armload of plover decoys.

There's no telling what those graceful, hand-carved birds would be worth on today's exotic decoy market. Wyman had owned them since his boyhood a half-century back. Their paint was faded, and Wyman showed me a couple of places where the wooden birds were pocked with the small, round holes left by shotgun-shell pellets.

Late the next afternoon we left his house in his well-traveled

Buick, taking along a .410 Winchester pump gun, a few shells loaded with No. 8s, and a burlap bag half-full of plover decoys. Without question both of us knew we were embarked on an illegal activity, but that aspect of the adventure was routine. Joe was left in his pen.

We went to the head of Three Mile Harbor, where Wyman kept his skiff with its one-cylinder inboard, loaded our gear, and set off down the channel for a small, uninhabited, sandy island near the breakwaters at the harbor entrance. It was not a remote island. Anyone standing on the town dock just across the channel could see and hear just about anything that went on over there. But that didn't give Wyman the slightest pause. We hauled the skiff ashore at the bar's northernmost end and, carrying our gear, walked to the southernmost point, the one that looked out over the broad reach of Three Mile Harbor.

Wyman set out seven or eight decoys, gently pushing each slim, single wooden leg into the soft sand at the water's edge. Then he and I sat behind a low driftwood log that, as far as I could tell, wasn't hiding either of us from anything. I wondered how any bird, including black-bellied plover, could fail to spot us perched there on the sand, one with a shotgun in his hand.

Then Wyman whistled. Such a clear, plaintive call. Three notes: the first high and long, the second much shorter and lower, the last note like the first, but not as sharp, a bit softer and touched with sadness. "*Weeee-urr-weee, weeee-urr-weee,*" over and over again, with a long pause in between.

And after five minutes the call came back to us from across the harbor, shimmering there in the sunset, hardly ruffled by the breezes of an early autumn evening. Wyman answered. The plover answered, this time louder, clearer.

Then I saw them, their long wings curved against the sky, a pair. They circled the decoys, calling, that plaintive whistling rippling in the still air. Wyman whistled back and the two plover set their wings to land. Wyman fired, one bird fell; I heard the click of the pump gun's action, then bang! The second bird went down in the shallow water a few feet off the shore.

As his knees creaked in unison, Wyman got to his feet and waded in to pick up the second plover; on his way back to the blind, he bent to get the first. "If you're trying for a double," he said, "get the farthest bird first. It's the one you have the best chance of losing."

He sat back down and whistled. Another few minutes, another answer, this time more than one. As a flock of five plover circled the decoys, Wyman dropped one, the last in the flock. "Maybe they'll come back," he said. And they did. Another bird down. "Johnny," he said, "you pick them up. I'll get the decoys. We don't want to overstay our welcome."

I was surprised at how large the birds seemed in my hand. Still warm and limp, they were a tender cargo, their plump breasts jet black, their backs pale and speckled. When I held out their wings, one tip in each hand, they were much longer than I expected. The total wingspan appeared to be almost two feet.

As I dropped the plover into the bag with the decoys, Wyman peered in. "Those will make a fine meal," he said." You ever try them?" I said no, but he didn't offer me one.

Back at the car, Wyman loaded the bag in the Buick's trunk along with his shotgun. Then he turned to me and said, "I sure missed that kind of shooting. Too bad they put the law on those birds."

A war and a few years later, when I was well along in my commercial fishing efforts, I found a patch of large quahogs in Napeague Harbor. The huge hard clams were bigger than softballs; it didn't take too many to fill a bushel basket. On autumn days when the surf was too rough for haul-seining, I'd go after those King Kong quahogs, tonging them from my skiff, which I kept pulled up on the beach. Back at home, I'd open the clams, put the meat in quart containers, and sell them for chowder, door-to-door. That way, I'd clear about five times as much for my work as I would have if I'd shipped the clams to Fulton Market in New York City.

I had that clam patch to myself. None of the other diggers thought those big quahogs were worth their time. They were down at Montauk Lake, bull-raking for littlenecks: the money clam. As I worked alone, shorebirds flew by, circled, and landed on the sand bar where Napeague flows into Gardiners Bay. They fluttered, picked here and there with their bills, and took off again, their wings beating in the stiff breeze.

They were restless, moved by migratory compulsions that would soon power their ascent into the high skies where they would fly through nights and days, thousands and thousands of miles to the other end of the earth, at Tierra del Fuego. These are the birds that see more sunlight than any other living creature, the "wind birds" as Peter Mathiessen calls them, the light-boned, heavy-breasted shorebirds whose wondrous navigations are still a mystery.

Whenever I saw a black-bellied plover among them, I would whistle as Wyman had, practicing to get my notes on key and the plaintive tone just right. I became good at it; plover would turn from their line of flight, search for the source, and fly toward me as I kept calling and they called back. Those wild birds and I were communicating, and I was thrilled by an exchange that allowed me such intimate contact with creatures that had always lived beyond my reach.

Ever since I first called to black-bellied plover I have learned the voices of other wild birds: crows, owls, warblers, night herons, black ducks, Canada geese, yellowlegs, killdeer, ospreys, quail, wild turkey—as many as I could master. I have called to birds all my life. No matter where I am, if a crow flies over, I greet him. Sometimes the birds wheel and return for a better look; they always acknowledge the call with a turn of their head or a few words of their own.

One fall morning when I left to go clamming I took a shotgun with me, a Parker twelve-gauge double that had been my father's quail gun. I shot two plover that day and took them home for dinner. When I plucked their feathers I discovered that the thin skin of their dark-fleshed breasts was stretched taut over a layer of fat unlike any I had ever seen. The ivory suet was more than a quarter-inch thick, a creamy blanket pulled snugly over the entire breast. It was fuel for the long flight every plover would make within the next few weeks.

Out of the oven and on our plates, those plover were delicious: firm, dark meat flavored with the rich and subtle taste of the wild. A memorable meal. My first and last. After that day alone at Napeague, I never killed another plover.

MUTE SWAN
(Cygnus olor)

∽

Our father was a large, sturdy man, big chested and broad shouldered. In photographs taken when he was young, he carries his size well; he is tall, lean, and imposing, his darkest of dark-brown eyes burning there in a clean-featured, impassive face that seems never to be smiling.

By the time I was a boy of ten or so, he had lost the edge of his leanness. Flesh gathered at his chest and midsection as he became heavy. He spent most of the rest of his life trying, unsuccessfully, to keep his increasing weight under control.

This considerable bulk—added to an already large man—was probably the chief reason why he and our mother had separate, but adjoining, bedrooms upstairs in the house on the east shore of Georgica Cove. Across to the west were the open fields and rather unkempt pastures of the Talmadge Farm: fields where big-boned workhorses rambled and, every so often, a small herd of Jersey cows would be turned out to graze.

That was the view from the northwest side of the long house. From our father's bedroom and bathroom, windows looked out across the upstairs porch, across the lawn, over the swath of cattails at the cove's rim, then across the water to the Talmadge fields. From there, the view extended to a gentle, wooded horizon that met the sky somewhere near an invisible Peconic Bay between Long Island's north and south forks. There was not a house or barn or water tank or any sign of manmade structure. Just the cove, its wreath of tall cattails swaying in the wind, and green woods and fields beyond. Quite a contrast in vistas for a man who spent so many of his days and nights in midtown Manhattan and Wall Street's canyons.

As a country boy, born in North Carolina's tobacco country near Winston-Salem, our father treasured that view from his upstairs rooms in the house on Georgica. He could see the entire cove and its complex wetlands and marshes. At the narrow channel that led from the cove to the larger main pond, fingers of muddy marsh were covered with a thick mat of cattails, some emerald green and growing, others brown and dying, their slow decay leaching organic sustenance to the pond. Channels just wide enough for a canoe or a small rowboat curled among those cattails, and there, in the farthest interior of the maze, was where a pair of mute swans nested early every spring.

Swans are long-lived, and the same pair nested in that same spot throughout my boyhood and early adolescence. We could tell they were the same swans because the male had a flaw at the tip of his orange-and-black beak—like a piece chipped from a much-used teacup. We called him Broken Bill and recognized him each time he came paddling to our small dock, his snowy chest puffed, his wings arched high above his back, his sinewy neck high and straight. Thus arrayed, he put on his dignified demonstration of strength and proclaimed his territorial domination of the cove, all its waters, its marshes, and especially the nest, where his mate of many years protected their brood.

That nest, so far back in the dense cattails, was a large mound about four or five feet in diameter, rising more than two feet above the water. The swan pair added new material each early spring and relined the heart of the nest with swan's down. As children, we were cautioned never to row the *Emma* into the swans' sanctuary. Those were prudent warnings.

Mute swans become very aggressive when they must defend their nesting grounds. These large, strong birds, with wingspans of better than six feet, have often attacked humans. Extending their muscular necks and beating their wings on the water's surface, angry swans fly just off the water directly at intruders. If this fails to deter them, the swans will make physical contact, hurling themselves at boats and boaters, beating at them with those sturdy wings, pecking, and lunging quite without fear.

Each summer we were dutifully told stories of other boys and girls who had been attacked by enraged swans. One girl, as we were always informed, had an arm broken by a blow from the wing of an attacker. These were definitely not the sedate and dignified birds that so often appeared in our storybooks.

Without question, Broken Bill was the most aggressive of Georgica's swans. He ruled the cove. And watching him fight for it again and again over the years made me a believer of all those stories about broken arms. They became very credible whenever I watched Broken Bill take on any of the several male rivals who came cruising into the cove from the big pond, where as many as thirty or forty pairs gathered every spring. As their numbers grew, they tried with increasing boldness to add the cove to their nesting grounds. It was, they recognized, one of the finest spots on all of Georgica to raise a swan family.

Which is why Broken Bill was challenged so often. Those battles began early in the morning when the winds were still and the cove's calm surface mirrored a brightening sky. With his belligerence apparent even at a distance, the contending male would paddle briskly through the narrow channel from the west and steam into the cove, doing whatever he could to make himself look fearsome, his puffed-up chest pushing aside water in a wide wake, his neck pulsing, curved back in an S that kept his beak ready to strike.

As soon as the intruder left the channel and entered the cove proper, Broken Bill would emerge full-speed from the cattails, charging directly at the challenger, legs pumping furiously as his webbed feet generated remarkable acceleration.

Often the sight of this aroused battleship was enough. Acting as if he realized for the first time that he had arrived where he was definitely not wanted, the visitor would spin and begin paddling even faster back where he had just come from. By then, Broken Bill would be following close behind, making quite certain the retreat was not a feint.

But there were those mornings when the invader stood his ground. Then the swan battle began; it was an awesome sight.

Meeting chest to chest with their wings beating mightily on the water and on each other, the fighters grappled for an advantage that would give one the leverage to hold the other's head and neck underwater. Swans do drown each other this way, and the birds do occasionally fight to the death. We never witnessed such mortal combat. Broken Bill was never defeated, and there were those moments when it seemed as if he could, if he chose, hold his opponent's head under long enough to drown him. But Broken Bill always relented. He would release the defeated invader, which would then leave the way he had come, trying as he went to salvage some dignity, shaking his wings into some semblance of order but paddling rather hastily toward the channel that marked the boundary of Broken Bill's territory.

For hours afterward, scattered swan feathers littered the cove like leaves blown from a snow-white tree.

As the vanquished challenger made his retreat, Broken Bill swam in the opposite direction, appearing for the moment to have lost all interest in what, just moments ago, had been a mortal struggle. But before he had gone far, Broken Bill would turn and begin the laborious process of taking flight. Every swan is apparently almost too heavy for its wingspan—formidable as that spread is—and must follow the same arduous procedure. First, they spread those great wings and begin flapping them so they strike the surface. At the same time, their webbed feet push hard and deep into the water, moving the bird forward.

After long moments of maximum physical effort, the swan's husky body begins to rise from the water. Soon it clears the surface and the bird is, literally, running across the water, its wings beating and its webbed feet pacing, one after the other, leaving spreading circles on the surface. The sound of those feet striking the water combines with the sharp slap of the wings to create a kind of liquid percussion like none heard anywhere but within earshot of a mute swan's takeoff. It has a rhythmic urgency, a sharp, upper-frequency slapping that's unique and unforgettable.

Under most circumstances, swans break free of the water before they've run a hundred feet. But when Broken Bill wanted to further humiliate his defeated and departing challengers, he stayed at surface level, letting the harsh slap of those great wings and the rap-rap of those webbed feet sound a kind of drum of doom in the ears of the vanquished. Often, those losers turned their heads on their long necks, looking apprehensively over their shoulders even as the wake of their anxious paddling spread wider when they advanced their escape speed.

Once the cove was cleared, Broken Bill swam its circumference, chest puffed, wings folded and arched high above his back in proclamation of his dominance and virility.

If our father was at home when the swans fought, he would step out on the upstairs porch to watch. In the early morning, wearing his bathrobe, he stood there alone at the rail, wondering if old Broken Bill still had the will and tenacity to do battle yet again. The two—that swan and our father—shared a kinship of responsibilities and roles.

When the swan eggs hatched, the newborn cygnets appeared on cove waters soon after their first breaths. Like yellow-brown, feathered puffballs on a tether, they trailed their mother wherever she cruised, gliding along slowly with effortless strokes of their webbed feet. Sometimes, it was difficult to see all the cygnets; they were so tiny and so fragile, and they clung so closely to their guardian. And with good reason: they were at their most vulnerable stage. The cove harbored more than its share of snapping turtles— large, black-backed, leathery shelled leviathans, some weighing more than fifty pounds. We saw them only when the females crawled onto dry land on their egg-laying missions. Otherwise, all we knew of the snapping turtle was the dark tip of its small nose poking like a black twig above the cove's surface. Their menace was submerged, out of sight.

And every now and then, one of those puffballs of a cygnet would lag a bit behind the family procession. One minute it would be part of an idyllic scene that could have been an illustration for *The Ugly Duckling.* In the next instant, it would vanish, pulled under so silently, so quickly we often wondered if we had truly seen it. We had. And we knew a snapping turtle had just had a snack.

After a few weeks, however, the cygnets grew as large as barnyard ducks, and slim fingers of white feathers began to poke through their dusky, childhood plumage. They were no longer in danger of being swallowed.

From his upstairs windows, our father kept close track of the brood's progress. He counted each of the newborns soon after they first appeared and each day thereafter he took a census, tabulating the year's survival rate. Soon he could identify each individual cygnet.

It was a kind of transposition for him, this constant interest in the cove's swan family. Born in Durham, North Carolina, in 1887, the oldest surviving son of a Methodist minister with nine children, our father left home for New York City when he was twenty-three, shortly after the minister died. As the eldest male, he felt it was his responsibility to do whatever he could to care for the family. Eleven years after he left the tobacco fields for one of the world's largest and most cosmopolitan cities, John Cole met Helen Dodd at a costume ball in Southampton. Dressed as a gypsy organ grinder, he took a monkey and a hand-cranked music box to the party, and through the entire evening Miss Dodd thought of him as an amusing musician hired by her hostess, Peg O'Brien.

The following afternoon, when he came walking toward the front entrance of the house on the cove, our mother, just seventeen, peered out a window and called to her mother, "Oh my goodness, here comes the organ grinder. Tell him I'm not here. Tell him he has to leave."

Less than a year later, on April 22, 1922, they were married at St. Bartholomews on Park Avenue. Our father was now inextricably committed to a life very different from the one he might have led if he had stayed in North Carolina, riding in the back of horse-drawn tobacco wagons along dusty, red-clay country roads. With a brokerage office on Wall Street, an east-side apartment in Manhattan, and the house in Easthampton, he must have thought he had realized every dream.

Yet he talked most often, and most wistfully, about those country roads and the South he had left behind. Often when Chick and I came down for breakfast, our father would be sitting alone in the dining room with the windows that overlooked the cove.

He would say, "Take a seat," and then tell us about the swans and their children. "Those cygnets aren't babies any more. They grow so fast. They have to. They've got just one summer. Then they are on their own. By the time the leaves begin to turn and we get our first frost, their parents won't be seeing much of them. Those young swans will be out in the world, alone, on their own."

He would pause and look straight at Chick and me, those unblinking, dark, dark eyes of his piercing our very souls. Shifting our skinny butts on those hard-seated dining-room chairs, we waited, mute, for more of the words we had heard many times before.

Leaning back in his chair, he'd reach into his jacket pocket for the Chesterfields he always carried. He smoked about a pack a day. When he pulled a cigarette from the package, he tapped one end of it on the polished table, tamping down loose tobacco so it stayed in place. The process never seemed to quite work; after he lit the cigarette he'd hold it out away from his face with one hand and reach up with the other to remove a bit of tobacco from his lip or tongue with the tips of his thumb and forefinger. He spoke while he smoked, so his words came out in puffs.

He'd say, "You boys don't have a care in the world here," gesturing toward the long window and the cove. "You've got nothing to do in this lovely place but enjoy it. You don't have to work at anything, not for a minute. You don't have a single chore.

"I grew up on a farm. I had jobs I had to do every day, and I was younger then than you are now. Those chores started early and ended late. I had chickens to take care of, eggs to gather, chicken houses to clean. There was a vegetable garden I had to weed, horse stalls to sweep.

"I was like those cygnets out there. I was just a boy and I was already learning how to get along on my own."

Looking out the window, he scanned the cove for any sign of the swans and their cygnets. Looking, looking, off there toward the northwest horizon, he found his brothers and sisters, ran with them down those red-clay roads, across the tobacco fields to the creek where they swam on dusty afternoons. Or on to the barn where they might find a wagon already hitched to a mule team, on its way to the general store where candy glowed in glass jars and red apples nested in wooden crates on dark, oiled floors. He missed that. He searched for it in the northwest sky.

"You and Chick, you've got to start learning to work. I won't always be here, you know. You'll be like those young swans out there. You'll be on your own. How do you think you'll do?"

Soon he would leave to go play tennis at the club. Chick and I watched him go, dressed in his cream-colored flannel trousers and white buckskin shoes. When he'd gone out the door, we'd sit there, silent, wondering what sort of chore we could do that would please our father.

We seldom came up with one, very seldom. But during those idyllic summer days, we would see the swan family cruising the cove and we would remember our father's dark, unforgiving eyes.

Much later, I learned that those large, white birds he so admired were not a natural presence in the cove, nor anywhere in the country. Their ancestors had been imported from Europe as ornaments for lily ponds on the estates of wealthy Americans who built great showplaces on Long Island and other northeast watering holes.

But for our father, Broken Bill and the swan family were there every summer to certify his past, to verify his values.

And, for all of my life, to remind me of my father.

AMERICAN ROBIN
(*Turdus migratorius*)

At the house on the cove, robins were on the lawn all summer long. They raised their numerous young in the dense, tangled branches of the high privet hedges that ran along the property's western boundary, where a bulkhead separated the sandy land from the cove's marshes. Often we found empty robin nests in the branches of that hedge, small circles of woven grass and mud that we carried indoors and kept on our bureau tops for the rest of the summer. The broken shells of the robin's brilliant, sky-blue eggs turned up at unexpected places on the property, and sometimes I found an almost perfect egg that I would show to our mother, Helen. I knew she would always tell me how much she loved that shade of blue.

Many early mornings when the lawn was damp with dew, Chick and I would watch from our upstairs windows while robins hunted for their breakfast. Skipping along on their thin sticks of legs, they would stop, cock their heads to one side, and then quickly poke their bills hard into the sod.

Our grandfather told us that whenever a robin cocked its head like that it was listening for the sound of a worm crawling underground. We believed him; there was nothing to disbelieve. For as we watched a robin cock its head, standing stock still, it would jab its bill into the grass and start yanking and tugging. Soon, a squirmy pink earthworm would stretch from the ground and then,

finally, lose its grip on life and end up thrashing in the tight vise of the robin's bill. Those worms, I've since learned, are the robin's meal of choice, and a diet enjoyed by few other birds. Which is good news for robins; there will, it seems, always be plenty of their favorite food.

By late June, the feeding adults would be trailed by their young of the year, fresh from their nests in our hedges. The children were always plump, it seemed, with speckled breasts instead of the solid red ones worn by their parents. They whined as they followed the grown-ups on their worm hunts, running up whenever a worm was yanked loose, hoping for a handout. It was such a comic sight that soon the entire household would be watching.

Our mother's formal garden was off the southwest corner of the house. Another privet hedge ran along its westernmost edge, and two wooden walls had been built on the south and north. They were thick, shingled on both sides to match the pale gray cedar shingles that covered the house. Broad white planks ran along the top of the walls, curving upwards over the two gated arches that were the garden's entrances, one on the north side, the other on the south. The house itself enclosed the rest, making that garden a kind of outdoor room, a private place.

At its center there was a bird bath framed by a circular bed of baby's breath. From there, the flower beds radiated like spokes, each separated by a narrow path of green grass. That garden belonged to our mother, who was there almost every day, working and cutting the fresh flowers she arranged so creatively in the vases she put in every room.

On a still August evening as the sun was about to set behind the Talmadge fields, I came through the garden's north gate with my BB gun—my first gun, given to me the previous Christmas when I was about to become ten years old. I'd come from the dock, where I'd been shooting at snapping turtle noses. Well, I told myself that's what they were; they could also have been sticks poking through the pond's still surface.

As I closed the gate I saw a robin across the garden, standing on top of the far wall on one of those broad white planks.

I put the BB gun to my shoulder, aimed at the bird, and pulled the trigger.

The robin dropped from the wall like a stone and fell into one of the flower beds.

"John!" my mother shouted, her voice ringing with shock and surprise. "You shot that robin. You killed that lovely bird. Why he was just up there on the wall looking so proud, and then you killed him. You just aimed that gun and killed him."

My mother had a strong, clarion voice and it filled the garden. I hadn't seen her standing there on the small porch at the corner of the house that overlooked the garden. Her angular, high-cheekboned face was pale in the low sun, her brown eyes wide against it, her white throat slim in one of the scarves she often wore to hide a slight scar left by thyroid surgery.

She wanted to take some action but couldn't think of just what to do, so she stood there, shouting, "How could you do such a thing?" over and over.

I trotted across the garden to find the robin. I never thought I could hit it when I fired. It was a long shot, the best I'd ever made. The robin was there at the bottom of the garden wall, lying quite still on the rich, dark soil.

As I reached to pick it up, my mother walked over, thin legs striding in her long skirt, communicating her distress. "Look at him," she said, "how handsome he is. That velvet black head, that lovely red breast. What a dapper fellow." Reaching out with her right hand she brushed the robin's breast with the tips of those fingers that I always thought were so extraordinarily long.

I was still proud of my shot. But my mother's shock and her poignant reprimands took the edge off my accomplishment. Holding that warm robin in my hand sent guilt tremors racing along every fiber of my consciousness. I grew more miserable by the second and knew I faced the prospect of miseries yet to come.

As I visualized those possible punishments, the robin moved in my hand, then spread quivering wings, trying to recover its equilibrium. I could see the skinned patch at the very top of its head where the BB had barely creased its skull.

I raised my hand high and in another moment, quickly and quite without apparent strain, the robin flew off toward the cove, over the gate, off into the setting sun. It was, I thought, a "happily ever after" end to a kind of fairy tale.

"Don't you ever shoot at a robin again," said my mother, walking back to the house. "Never, ever again."

Over the many years since then, as I've watched robins on every lawn at every house we've ever lived, I've decided they cock their heads to see better, to bring one of their keen eyes to bear more directly on their quarry. But that's only my theory. Our grandfather may have been right.

OSPREY

(Pandion haliaetus)

The osprey has been part of my life longer than any other bird. Whenever I consider which bird I would elect to become when my soul is recycled, I choose the osprey. Which should not surprise anyone who knows me, even casually. The osprey is a fish hawk. It lives close to the water, follows the sun, and spends its days catching fish. Which is exactly how I live when I'm not working to pay bills.

I was just nine when Chick and I were sent to our very first boarding school: Friends Academy in Locust Valley, Long Island. That's young enough to get seriously homesick, which is one reason I'll never forget our grandparents and their early spring arrivals at the school door. They stopped by to take us along on their weekend trips to their house on Georgica Pond.

In the early spring, Georgica spills across the narrow strip of beach that separates its southernmost end from the Atlantic. As the pond water floods the sand it cuts a deep channel that soon clouds with fragments of the pond's eelgrass, schools of minnows, and small crustaceans being swept out to sea. When, at last, the pond sheds all of its accumulated excess, the process reverses and at high tide some of the ocean's anadromous migrants crowd into the channel on their seasonal spawning runs.

Of those migrants, the alewife outnumbers all others. The foot-long, silver fish, one of the herring family, swims in great, bright

schools. Such is the urgency of its spring mission that it pays little attention to its personal safety; vast numbers of alewives were once scooped silver from their tidal runs by men with nets who used the fish for fertilizer or pickled them in brine for future lobster bait.

Once in the pond, the alewives apparently swim into every cove, including the one in front of the house that was our grandparents' during those long-ago years. Every osprey in the neighborhood knew the fish were there, and on those bright days when spring light flooded the greening landscape with its almost unbearable brilliance, I could count as many as twenty of those fish hawks circling against the blue sky above us.

I watched them for hours and could have watched them the entire day, they were so perfect at what they did. They are a species unto themselves, these fishing birds. There is no other hawk that gets almost all its sustenance from the water. Gliding on its five-foot wingspan, circling on thermals, fifty feet or more above our cove, the osprey's keen, raptor eyes could see alewife backs wriggling like eelgrass beneath Georgica's rippled surface. Once a single fish was chosen, the bird would fold its wings so they paralleled its body, tip into a steep dive, and fall from the sky like a feathered stone. Just before it struck the water with a great plume of a splash, the osprey would rear back, extending its talons far in front of its breast.

Vanishing into the white water of its impact, the bird would submerge for a long moment, its entire body down there in the dark of the pond. My breath always stopped as I watched, waiting, until the bird's wings emerged, sweeping against the surface in urgent, powerful strokes. On quiet mornings, I could hear the sibilance of those emergings. Then, almost every time, the osprey would flap clear, and in its talons, the head facing front, an alewife quivered. Caught there for its brief eternity in long, curved claws, the fish was held fast by the tiny spines that cover the undersides of the osprey's feet, giving them the rough texture that ensures an unbreakable grip.

Every now and then a single osprey would drop down to water level and fly along, dragging its feet on the surface, leaving a line of darker blue in its wake. As a boy watching, I assumed the bird had seen a fish, then changed its mind about making a dive. Later I learned the osprey does not often make that sort of misjudgment; those fish hawks were dragging their feet to wash off the slime that had accumulated after the capture of several alewives.

Twenty-some years after those spring weekends by Georgica I got to know the osprey on even more intimate terms. That was during my commercial fishing days, when I worked a few months on Gardiners Island, the place that hosts the largest number of nesting osprey on the entire northeast coast—as many as four hundred or five hundred birds and more than two hundred nests during the year I was there. The birds were part of every one of my days as an evaluator of the island's shellfish resource, work that kept me on or near the island's three salt ponds from first light until dark.

As I stood up to my waist in one of the ponds, scratch-raking for clams or searching for oyster spat, the high-pitched whistling call of the osprey was always in my ears. Circling overhead, they called to me and to each other as they hunted for the fish they needed to feed their two or three downy chicks. Sprawling in huge nests of twigs, mud, grass, old bones, seaweed, and occasionally a length of rotting manila rope, those chicks would stand and crane their scrawny necks whenever a fish-bearing parent approached. The whistling calls would get louder still, and I could see the adult bird's head bobbing as it tore the fish into bite-size strips for the fledglings. I learned to whistle shrilly enough to imitate the ospreys, and every now and then a fish hawk would answer my call with one of its own.

Osprey nests were part of the Gardiners Island landscape from one end to the other, and when my job there ended and my new family and I lived on the Long Island mainland, just across the bay from the island, I found myself looking for more nests as I traveled from Greenport to Shelter Island, Sag Harbor, Napeague, Montauk, and each of the other East End fishing villages. I had, I realized, bonded with the osprey and would be looking for it for the rest of my days.

A few years after my summer on Gardiners, the alarm sounded for the osprey, the eagle, and other birds of prey that consumed fish, birds, and animals at the top of the food chain. Because they contained high-level concentrations of the pesticide DDT, the very creatures that sustained a raptor's life were also packed with poison. In less than a decade, the number of active osprey nests on Gardiners was cut by half. It was that disaster, along with Rachel Carson's eloquent book *Silent Spring,* that first raised my environmental consciousness and became the foundation of my personal values and opinions. The osprey changed my life; that's not an exaggeration.

In the late 1950s, I moved from Long Island to Maine, where we have lived most of our years since. During its brief and brilliant summers, the Maine coast is home to more ospreys than any other northeastern habitat except Long Island. So the bond between us has not been broken: the swift-winged bird of my boyhood still calls to me each spring when it returns to the Maine coast during the third week of March. During my Georgica years, March 23 was the date I knew I could count on seeing an osprey, back from its winter migration south of the ice line. March 23 is my father's birthday, another link between me and the fish hawk.

The birds are back, too, from the DDT-induced tumble toward extinction, now that the pesticide has been banned. All of us—I hope—learned a lesson in the process. Each year osprey nests in Maine are surveyed, and each year for the past decade the news has been good: more young hatched, more fledglings taking wing, more adults returning the following March.

On a fine September day when I was scalloping off Gardiners Island in those splendid fishing years of the early 1950s, I watched as an osprey dove on a school of big bluefish. Just as I had as a boy, I held my breath after the splash—the moment when the bird disappeared beneath the white plume of its entry. After a long moment, the osprey's powerful wings beat on the water but gained no altitude. Then that fish hawk vanished, pulled beneath the waters that never opened for it again, even though I waited there watching for at least fifteen minutes.

I had read that ospreys sometimes get their talons locked in the shoulders of a fish too large for the taking. In these encounters, death claims both fish and bird. I hold the image of that Gardiners Bay struggle clear in my memory; it has not dimmed a single degree over all these years.

DOUBLE-CRESTED CORMORANT
(Phalacrocorax auritus)

Like the osprey, the cormorant has been a bird of most of my years. Unlike the osprey, however, this other catcher of fish has never scored high marks when it comes to grace, noble ferocity, good looks, or artistry on the wing. Indeed, until I softened up in my senior years, the dear old cormorant seemed to me to be a comic, somewhat unattractive bird; I have come to love it only because it's always there to greet me whenever I'm on or near the water, no matter where that water might be.

And from what I have learned about these birds, I could travel the oceans of the world and there it would be: some member of the cormorant family—scrawny, sloppy, and ungainly, but nevertheless ubiquitous and out there ready to say good morning whether I sailed the China Sea, the Bay of Biscay, or the Bahia de Sechuro.

Which you might expect from a global family of at least thirty species. For the record, the double-crested cormorant of the U.S. eastern seaboard is the bird that I have come to know so well over some sixty years. And perhaps it is my own lifelong guilt that corrodes our relationship, for during the early stages of my waterfowl hunting career, I shotgunned countless numbers of cormorants as casually as you might slap a mosquito that's biting your neck.

In those times, back in the late 1930s and throughout the 40s,

killing cormorants was not a crime, not legally. Like the crow and many species of hawks, cormorants were not protected by state or federal regulations of any kind. It was their skill as fish eaters that earned them this universal condemnation. Sporty salmon anglers hated the cormorant because it consumed, they firmly believed, incredible numbers of Atlantic salmon smolt. Commercial fisherman hated the cormorant because they believed that it destroyed entire populations of infant striped bass, shad, weakfish, and other anadromous species. Growing up in a culture of such unanimously negative opinions gave me all the arguments I needed to talk myself into believing that every cormorant I killed was justifiable avicide committed in the name of protecting our marine resources.

Cedar Point is a thin sand spit that pokes north into Gardiners Bay almost to Shelter Island. Like arms extended in an embrace, the point and the island enclose a large body of water off Sag Harbor, and in the fall, cormorants gathered there during the day to work the fish traps. Each dawn they flew in, each evening they flew out, and both flights crossed the narrow strip of beach halfway along Cedar Point.

With my grandfather's ten-gauge—a full-choke, double-barreled shotgun with 32-inch, twist-steel barrels and two hammers that had to be cocked each time I fired—I would walk the gated two-mile dirt road out to the point and scoop a depression in the coarse beach sand. In the morning, I got there before sunrise, often with my brother Chick, Harry Steele, and other duck hunting friends who shot cormorants as a kind of warm-up for the season that was a few weeks off.

We called the birds shags or nigger geese; I'm pretty sure we didn't know their ornithological name. As dawn colored the eastern sky in back of Gardiners Island, we'd see long, wavering, dark lines against the pale sky, strands of black thread rippling in a wind. When they came closer, we could pick out individual birds and decide which would be the most likely to cross within range. Shags are sloppy fliers. Rocking back and forth in the wind, flailing their skinny wings, they have none of the bullet-like, straight-trajectory flight characteristics of most waterfowl. They dip, waver, and flap around the sky like lost leaves in a gale.

Hit with a magnum load of number-four pellets shot from a long-barreled, full-choke gun, those shags folded like torn kites and fell spinning from the sky. We never kept count, but then we never killed too many. Even in those days shotgun shells were costly for school boys on their summer vacations.

A few days after Pearl Harbor, I enlisted in the Army Air Corps. When I stripped for my physical the medical officer was startled by the size of the black-and-blue bruise sprawled over my right shoulder and collarbone. "Were you in an accident?" he asked.

"No, just gunning," I explained, and told him about that ten-gauge with its straight stock.

After the war, I shot one or two shags before I quit for good. It began to seem quite wrong to kill a bird and let it lie where it fell. And a few years later, the gawky birds were protected, along with hawks, by the federal government.

On the Maine coast, not far from our home, double-crested cormorants nest on rocky islands and raise their young there. The tops of the rocks are white with guano; the featherless infant birds stretch naked heads and necks that look like prehistoric lizards whenever their parents fly in and regurgitate the fish they have caught and packed in their craws. In such surroundings, there can be no doubts about the link between these birds and the flying reptiles of the Jurassic Period 180 million years ago. Cormorants are an ancient race indeed.

Once, sailing my Hobie Cat in Middle Bay on a brilliant September morning, I cruised right over a cormorant. On a downwind heading, the single sail at right angles to the twin hulls, I lay on the canvas deck with my head over the forward edge so I could look straight down into the clear water. A cormorant dove quite a ways off, and I was startled to see it just a few moments later there in the clear water, swimming some six feet directly beneath me, its webbed feet paddling with fierce energy, its neck and head straining forward as its dark, streamlined torso shot ahead like a squeezed watermelon seed. For a bird so ungainly in the air, the cormorant submerged is as sleek, speedy, and graceful as a seal. If I had seen it first underwater, I might have thought it beautiful forever.

Since my ten-gauge days, the cormorant's diet has been the focus of considerable research. What we believed as teenagers about the bird's appetite for game fish has been proven wrong. Cormorants feed largely on "trash" fish, we are informed, and, in the process, aid the overall balance of the marine environment. Add this virtue to their incredible production of some of the world's finest organic fertilizer, and you may justly condemn me for whatever losses I caused the cormorant community back in my heedless teens. Ignorance can be costly.

Over the years since, I have come to love this ungainly bird. During our time in Key West and on my frequent fishing trips from there as far west as the Marquesas, I saw cormorants each day: perched atop buoys; diving in the distance, the silver trail of their wakes often fooling me into thinking I saw fish; sitting on bridges or the bones of derelict boats; and flying at me out of the sunrise just as they had at Cedar Point. And I see them still each spring, summer, and fall here on the Maine coast, where I've marked their arrivals and departures on our calendars every year for the past two decades.

In every life there are icons that connect you with your childhood, those days of exuberance, adrenaline, and thoughtless excess. For me, the cormorant is one of the most dependable, and I am delighted and grateful each time we meet. Still, I often can't help smiling at its clumsiness on the wing. Which is, I suppose, one of the reasons why my affections have grown through all these years.

TURKEY VULTURE
(Cathartes aura)

❧

The turkey vulture—the large, dark scavenger much better known as a buzzard—is often the first bird seen and noticed by a child of the South. That's because the turkey vulture is ubiquitous in southern skies. At any given moment of the day, a person in Virginia (and from there south to Key West) can look up and find a turkey vulture soaring high above. The great, broad wings, almost as large as an eagle's, are outstretched, motionless as the bird rides the thermals, its keen eyes probing the distant landscape for carrion, garbage, or a crippled animal or bird.

Southern fables have been woven around the buzzard; southern jokes feature it as a character; southern superstitions spring from the turkey vulture's associations with the dead and the dying. My father, born and raised in North Carolina, was a fine storyteller. He knew the dialects and the folk tales and the familiar birds and animals of the South. One of his favorite tales (I heard it many times) was about a buzzard that had gotten so rich he had given up his old friends and moved to a large estate on Long Island's north shore. There he had a full staff of servants, including a butler with a British accent. One morning Mr. Rabbit delivered a truckload of fertilizer for the estate's broad, green lawn. He rang the doorbell and the butler answered.

"Is my old friend Buzzard here?" said Mr. Rabbit.

"Mr. Buzz*ard* is out in the yard," the butler replied, looking down his long nose and putting the accent on the "ard" and stretching it out so it rhymed with yard.

"Well," said the rabbit, "tell him Mr. Rabb*it* [accent on the "it"] is here with the shit."

The concept of a nouveau-riche buzzard is the heart of the story; in the South the turkey vulture may be appreciated for its duties as a scavenger, but it is not high on anyone's list of desirable birds, like the cardinal or the mockingbird. But, in fact, the buzzard is a remarkable and ancient bird, a survivor of the ice ages, little changed in a million years. Its aeronautic design, which fits a six-foot wing span onto a very light skeletal frame, gives the bird highly efficient soaring abilities.

Which is how I first got to know the turkey vulture: it soared across my school days. Because our father wanted my brother and me to know something of the South where he was raised, Chick and I were sent to boarding school at Woodberry Forest in Orange, Virginia, a small town in the Blue Ridge foothills near the state's northern boundary. Set on a hill that rose from the Rapidan River and surrounded by red-clay farm country, Woodberry was—and still is—in the heart of excellent buzzard habitat.

Almost all of our classrooms had high windows, and as I sat at my desk in each of those rooms for five long school years, I spent much of my time daydreaming and watching buzzards soar. They were there almost every day, fall, winter, and spring. I envied them their freedom and their genius for riding the wind. Often I would keep track of the number of times they would move their wings during one of the school's standard fifty-minute periods. There were days when the thermals must have risen to perfection and the turkey vultures rode them more efficiently than any glider pilot. Circling, rising, circling, drifting downward then rising up again, never flapping their wings once. It seemed a miracle to me that those huge, dark birds could stay aloft, guiding their effortless flight with subtle movements of their stout primary feathers at the very ends of those long, broad wings.

Trying to understand how the buzzards so mastered the skies

was one of the reasons (one of many) why I never distinguished myself as a student. Those were not my happiest years, but the soaring hundreds of buzzards I tracked year after year are still there in my schoolboy memories. And I never really linked those high fliers with the large, hulking, clumsy black birds I sometimes saw hopping and flapping off some country road where a possum or coon carcass lay near the centerline.

Since my first year at Woodberry, turkey vultures have persistently extended their northern range. Sixty years ago, very few people in Maine, where I've lived for most of the past thirty-five years, could have counted on seeing a buzzard in Down East skies. But these days, after the open fields have shed the snows of winter, turkey vultures—or "TVs," as bird-watchers call them—are fairly frequent visitors. And, yes, each time I see one I'm back in Latin class wishing I was soaring.

Until our recent years in Key West, I have always considered Orange, Virginia, to be turkey vulture headquarters. And I never expected to discover flocks of several hundred buzzards circling at the very southernmost end of the hundred-mile curve of islands that are the Florida Keys. But one January morning I looked up at the soft skies of that semitropical day and there were more turkey vultures and their black vulture cousins than I had ever seen. And in the last spot I had ever expected such an encounter.

And when I say hundreds I mean perhaps a thousand, maybe more. It was impossible to make an accurate count; that would have been like trying to tabulate the number of bees in a swarm. The birds looked like a column of smoke rising on an unseen wind. Around and around and around they soared, silent, gliding, turning like leaves pulled aloft in a slow-motion whirlwind.

On that first meeting I thought some biological disaster had occurred at sea, a toxic shock that had killed tens of thousands of fish whose bodies now floated toward shore, where this vast congregation of buzzards waited for the meal of their lives. But, as I later learned from discussions with Key West ornithologists Bill and Fran Ford, the great buzzard gathering is an annual get-together. "Kettling" is the name birders have given to the behavioral quirk that brings such a mass of vultures together over this one small dot of an island between the Atlantic and the Gulf.

No one is certain of the reasons why. It is something turkey vultures and black vultures do in winter when they reach this continental outpost on their southern migrations. As long as no one can explain such behavior with scientific certainty, I propose a theory of my own: After their steady migratory flight south along the Atlantic coast all the way from Maine and other New England states, the buzzards run out of land when they reach Key West. There is nothing beyond them but the considerable expanse of the blue Caribbean.

So the big birds hesitate, trying to decide whether they should spend their winter in the Keys or press on toward South American havens. "What do we do now?" the vultures ask their flight leaders. And judging from the kettling that goes on, those leaders reply, "Keep circling. We'll think of something."

Snowy Owl
(*Nyctea scandiaca*)

It is a terrible thing to kill a bird the very moment you first meet. I was alone on a small sand spit more than fifty years ago when I shot a snowy owl with my grandfather's ten-gauge. I have regretted the killing ever since. And I can still see that great, white bird gliding silently straight at me, arrived from the mystery of all I did not know.

Early in the fall of 1941 I motored in a borrowed skiff to Cartwright Shoals, a sand spit that runs west from the southernmost tip of Gardiners Island. The half-mile gap between the shoals and the island is a passage for many sea ducks, cormorants, and the occasional migrating waterfowl. I went there often to shoot shags and scoter; both species traded back and forth off Cartwright almost every autumn day.

It is a lonely, windswept place, nothing but sand, beach grass, scattered driftwood, and the sea-beaten blanks of wrecks that have foundered on those treacherous shallows over the centuries. There are stories of gold coins being found after storms, coins a violent sea has plundered from Captain Kidd's treasure chests, which are buried, as three centuries of local legend testify, somewhere beneath Cartwright's shifting sands.

I had heard those legends many times before that late September afternoon when I pulled the skiff ashore at Cartwright's western tip. I planned to walk to the small island's eastern end and lie

there on the sand, waiting for a passing shot at any cormorants that flew past on their way home from their working day on the bay.

I had taken just a few steps from the skiff when up from a small rise directly before me this startling, large, silent, white bird appeared, no more than thirty feet from where I walked. I stopped as if I'd hit a wall. For a split second I thought the bird's talons were extended toward me . . . or do I rationalize? Have I told this to myself over all the years?

I snapped the loaded shotgun to my shoulder and fired. The bird (I had no idea what species it might be) banked sharply and glided toward the island's other end. Certain I hadn't missed, I was stunned. The bird should have fallen. I ran after it and found it at the brink of the bay, its great wings spread on the damp sand and seaweed.

It was an owl, I knew, after I picked it up, turned it over, and could see its large, round head, curved beak, and round, yellow eyes, staring directly at me. But such an owl, larger than any I had ever seen and almost pure white from head to tail, a startling white, paler than any seagull, brilliant in the September sun. Its feathers were soft, thick, dense enough to hide the blood seeping from its wounds.

What had I done?

I wrapped the owl in my jacket and put it in the boat. When I reached the beach at Devon and put the skiff back where it belonged, I drove to Doc Helmuth's with the bird on the seat beside me.

"A snowy owl," Doc said as I began unwrapping the carcass. "No other owl looks like this one. And a male, too. They are almost pure white."

He put yet another one of his hundreds of ornithological texts in my hands, this one on birds of prey. I learned that the snowy owl is a fairly well known and often seen resident of the Arctic tundra, where it nests and lives most of its life. It hunts by day and will kill lemmings, mice, moles, rats, rabbits, snowshoe hares, and small birds. If those are not on the premises, it will attack pets and poultry. When these and other prey are extremely scarce, this owl will take fish from the surface of the Arctic's icy waters. A courageous but wary bird in its Arctic habitat, the snowy owl is hunted by Eskimos, who will also steal its eggs if they find a nest on the tundra.

When I showed the trophy—as I thought of it then—to my parents, my mother was taken with the owl's fierce beauty, and off it went to a New York City taxidermist to be mounted. For several years after that, the great white bird glared at Chick and me from its eternal perch on a gnarled pine branch, its wings spread high in a V above its perfect snowy breast.

Then the house was sold, the furniture shifted, the family fractured as children became adults, moved away, married, and began other families. By then, the snowy owl had dimmed to a dirty gray; neglect and little understanding of how its feathers could be properly cleaned had robbed it of its majesty. It was decided we should donate it to New York City's Natural History Museum, which accepted it with thanks and where it still is today, as far as I know. I saw it once, under glass in some far corner of that vast museum, and its grandeur had been restored. The museum had done a splendid job of cleaning and grooming.

The bird was still a part of my life, however, not only in my memory, but as the subject of a fine portrait of it painted by Ellen Barry, a friend of my mother's. She gave the painting to me, and had so inscribed it in a delicate script painted with a fine-tipped brush in the lower right-hand corner. That painting hung over the mantel in the sun porch of the house on the dunes in East Hampton for many more years, and I never thought about taking it anywhere else. Time enough, I told myself, after the house was sold or both parents were dead,: an eventuality I never considered possible in those years.

But the house was sold, and the painting with it. I was never consulted. That has rankled a bit over the years, but with nowhere near the intensity of the guilt I still feel for having shot that splendid creature from the skies it patrolled with such awesome majesty.

Every several years, as I have since learned, snowy owls leave their tundra homes and fly south, sometimes as far as Virginia and, rarely, the Gulf states. Although no one is absolutely certain of the causes of these aberrant, winter migrations, there is a kind of consensus that these elegant hunters are forced to leave home because there is no food to be found. Arctic rodent population cycles can dip to almost zero, leaving the snowy with no choice: it's fly south, where there will be more food, or stay in the far north and starve.

Since that day on Cartwright I have seen migrant snowy owls several times. One caused a considerable stir in Brunswick, Maine, after we moved there. That bird perched atop the roof of a downtown department store, where it had discovered a hapless flock of pigeons. Photographers crowded the street, the owl's picture appeared on front pages, and area ornithologists were interviewed. That snowy stayed in the neighborhood for several days, and I was one of the crowd that tracked it during its visits. It would sit there atop one building or another, perched haughtily, quite unawed by its audience, which it regarded with those fierce, yellow eyes. Each time I saw it, I thought about that day on Cartwright Shoals and wished yet again that I had never killed that great white bird.

MOURNING DOVE
(*Zenaida macroura*)

~

Each year, so I'm informed by reliable sources, some twenty million mourning doves are shot and killed by hunters in most of the lower forty-eight states. Maine, I am pleased to note, is not one of them. Although there are regular efforts to legislate a Maine dove-hunting season, thus far they have not succeeded. In my opinion, those who argue that this gentle bird should have at least one sanctuary make the most telling case.

After all, it's not as if an inveterate dove shooter doesn't have a variety of opportunities. From California to the Carolinas, and Texas to Montana, dove seasons follow one after the other. A committed shooter could spend three or four months doing little else but knocking down doves if he had the time, the inclination, and the money to pay for travel, licenses, and thousands of shotgun shells.

And I'll bet ten-to-one that there are dove shooters who do just that. These birds, after all, are excellent fliers—fast, tricky, difficult to anticipate. They are plentiful and delicious and they can be shot at with no more effort than it takes to stand at the shaded edge of a grainfield. I know; I've done it.

It's a memory the bird itself has helped to keep fresh in my mind's eye. After Maine's long winters, the early spring call of the mourning dove is a blessed verification that the sun will soon shine longer, the snows will melt, and the first crocus will bloom. It is a

haunting sound, this *cooo-cooo-cooo,* and I suppose it is mournful in its way, but I have never thought it so. It is, after all, a wooing call, a love song, properly recognized by the Old Testament poet who wrote:

> Rise up my love, my fair one, and come away.
>
> For, lo, the winter is past, and rain is over and gone;
>
> The flowers appear on the earth; the time of the singing of birds has come, and the voice of the turtle is heard in the land.
>
> *Song of Solomon 2:10–12*

Whenever I read those lines I wonder how many dove shooters know they are swinging on a Biblical bird; these days almost no one calls it a turtledove.

It is a lovely creature, more beautiful in the hand than most observers could possibly imagine when they see it perched on a telephone wire or on the ground, picking up grains of sand for its crop with that jerky head motion that's so characteristic of the dove family. There is a creaminess to the breast feathers touched with a most delicate shade of pink, an unexpected opalescent tint that you might never notice from afar. With its graceful, pointed wings; a long tail fringed with white; and tiny, coral-red feet, this bird that so often appears dressed in drab olive-brown is almost exotic.

Its wing beats are rapid and make a wonderful whistling sound that identifies the mourning dove even when it can't be seen. In Maine, because they are not hunted, they have become back-door birds and will stay through the winter if there's a well -stocked feeder handy. We have had at least two pairs of mourning doves close by our back porch through the worst winters, although after an ice storm or blizzard they often looked to me as if they might be regretting their decision not to make the flight to Maryland's Eastern Shore or the dunes of Hatteras.

Like many birds of my years, the mourning dove has extended its range significantly farther north during my lifetime. As a boy I heard that *coo-coo*ing call as I awakened on those spring mornings in that house by Georgica Pond. A few years later, when I lived year-round on Long-Island's east end, doves were never seen during the winter. But now, here they are in Maine, huddled in the shelter of our woodsheds as snowdrifts build against our barn door.

No one has yet fully explained the reasons for this persistent and well documented push to the north by a number of bird species. Whatever the cause, I'm delighted that mourning doves pay us a visit almost every day of the year. They are such gentle, lovely, light-winged fliers. And here in Maine where they are never hunted, they have come to trust us. Which, when you think about their twenty million brethren that are killed each year, is quite remarkable.

PASSENGER PIGEON
(*Ectopistes migratorius*)

In 1808, the Ohio ornithologist Arthur Wilson observed a flock of passenger pigeons near Frankfort, Kentucky, and estimated their numbers to be "at least 2,230,272,000 individuals."

In 1911, writing in his *Handbook of Birds* (the first bird book I owned, given to me by Doc Helmuth) Frank Chapman reports, "I learned that a female passenger pigeon is said to have been shot at Bar Harbor, Maine, in the summer of 1904. It was mounted in July of that year by J. Bert Baxter, a taxidermist of Bangor who received it in the flesh. The present whereabouts of this specimen are unknown."

On the same page as the illustration of the mourning dove in Roger Tory Peterson's *A Field Guide to the Birds* there is a portrait of a passenger pigeon's head. Framed by a circle, the portrait is footnoted: "Extinct."

WHITE-WINGED SCOTER
(*Melanitta fusca*)

~∾

The bluebird is New York's state bird and thus Long Island's also. But Long Island is nothing like the rest of the state and should, I believe, have its own bird. If such a vote is ever taken, I nominate the white-winged scoter and believe it will win any such contest hands-down.

Why? Well, for one thing, it's an open-water bird, a sea duck. As such, it spends most of its life either flying over, diving deep into, or paddling on the surface of the full expanse of Long Island Sound, its several bays, and the entire reach of the open Atlantic from Montauk Point to Sandy Hook.

It's a bird that lives from and on the salt sea. Each year more white-wings gather on the waters off Long Island than any other waterfowl. Symbolically and actually, this most abundant member of the scoter family is a true representative of one of the island's most irreplaceable natural treasures: the sea around it.

And, like that island itself, the scoter is a tough, resilient bird that can take a great deal of punishment. A sociable creature, it likes nothing better than gathering in large flocks for its own brand of shellfish buffet. And it's a fine parent that takes excellent, long-term care of its offspring, spending most of its summers teaching them how to swim, fly, and find food.

Large, with a stocky, almost volleyball-size torso, the scoter is padded with thick, coal-black feathers that keep it warm and waterproof in the chilliest of seas. Its wings are each marked with tidy white patches, and the males have a white accent mark beneath each eye. Both male and female have large, very strong, knobby bills designed for yanking mussels and other bivalves from their beds and then crushing their shells.

Scoters dive to fifteen feet and deeper, can stay submerged for almost twenty minutes, and, during their dive, often flap their wings for added propulsion so they literally fly underwater. When they fly above it, especially in the fall as they mass for their winters offshore, their flocks are stretched single-file along September's sharp horizons. Those long, wavering, dark lines against the sharp-blue equinoctial sky are sewn forever in the patchwork of my seasonal memories.

Why is it that September has such a hold on our souls? For me, the white-wing is part of the answer. I can still hear the fragile, flute-like whistle of the beating of a thousand scoter wings as the flocks skimmed the rise and fall of each Atlantic swell in the Septembers of my youth.

And when the ducks settled on those offshore waters, their rafted congregations of ten thousand or more became a great, dark coverlet spread on the sparkling sea. Those flocks were a signal to all of us who went "coot shooting" in Gardiners Bay each autumn. Gunners then and now refer to each of the three scoter species by the generic name *coot* (no relation to the true coot, a rather simple-minded bird of the inshore marsh).

Chick and I would haul our grandparents' skiff, the *Emma*, from her Georgica berth to Promised Land, where the Smith Meal Company's rendering plant converted thousands of tons of menhaden into oil, fish meal, and other byproducts. There on those briny docks saturated with menhaden's rich, oily smell, the Edwards brothers kept a small general store for the crews who worked the boats that netted the fish factory's raw materials. Captain Sam Edwards berthed his dragger there, and it was he who organized and led each coot-shooting expedition, along with his brother, Dr. Dave Edwards, and various Edwards kin.

In the darkness of pre-dawn, an assembly of skiffs was made

fast to the towline of Captain Sam's dragger, and the wavery procession would be towed north across Gardiner's Bay to the Cartwright Shoals, the scene of my mortal meeting with the snowy owl. One by one the skiffs would drop off and anchor at what was judged to be a safe gunshot apart. Shotguns must have had a shorter range in those days; it always seemed to me that Chick and I could easily be stung with No. 4 bird shot if either of our coot-shooting neighbors got careless.

When each skiff was in place, the pass between Cartwright and Gardiners Island looked a bit like a marine picket line. No bird, however elusive, could get through the gap without being in range of at least one or two guns. Crouched down almost flat on our skiff, we each watched the open water off bow and stern. Every few moments or so, when the shooting was good, flights of white-wings in formations of twos and threes came straight at us a few feet above the water: round, black torpedo planes bearing down. Guns roared, shot hissed on the surface, some scoters fell, most zipped through the gauntlet. For an hour or so during the sunrise flight the shooting was fast, confused, and exciting. Our adrenaline pumped; one gunner pumped a bit too much and blasted a clean hole through the bottom of his skiff.

The scoter's dark breast meat—rich, a bit tough, and fully flavored—was stripped in filets from the birds once they were brought home. Dr. Dave pickled his, packing them in mason jars with bay leaves. My first knowledge of the white-wing's existence came on an early boyhood visit to the doctor's office. I'd fallen and cut my leg along the shinbone just below the knee, and the good doctor decided to stitch my wound then and there in his office. Trying not to look at the needle, I stared up, off into the distance; there on a high shelf along two sides of the room were jar after jar of pickled scoter breasts as neatly arranged as any prize-winning exhibit at a county fair.

I'm sure there aren't many gunners left who pickle their scoters, but I do know that every so often during the sea-duck hunting season a string of skiffs stretches from Cartwright to Gardiners just as it has for most of the twentieth century.

CANADA GOOSE
(Branta canadensis canadensis)

In the world of sea, marsh, pond, and beach that was the world of my most memorable adventures as a boy and young man, the birds that lived there were my constant companions. Indeed, they were often pivotal players in the melodramas of my youth. The osprey, the snowy owl, the plover—each of them occupied large spaces in my life; so large that it may be difficult for others to comprehend the intensity of my feelings for the feathered creatures that were so often the focus of my days and my dreaming.

But of the birds that lived in my consciousness, none was a more constant companion than the Canada goose. It had to do with the timing of those weekend trips to the house on Georgica Pond—the wonderful escapes our grandparents allowed us when they pulled up to the Friends Academy front steps on Friday afternoons and carried me and Chick off in that gleaming black Packard. Off on the miraculous sixty-mile drive that left one wretched world behind and arrived at a place of enchantments and wonders.

Those trips began in early March, as soon as the risk of freezing seemed remote (the house was built on posts, and each October the pipes were drained). Just as our grandparents waited for an end to winter, so did the Canada geese. Our arrivals at Long Island's easternmost end coincided, and those meetings were some of the most emotional and memorable of all my school years.

Lying awake just after dawn in a room still brittle with winter's persistent chill, snug under heavy, reassuring blankets, I would feel and hear the rattle from the kitchen one floor below our bedroom as our grandfather shook down ashes in the coal stove that warmed water in the tall copper boiler. I often heard, too, the shrill, melodious, and unmistakable call of Canada geese as they began their new day after a night of rest on the pond just beyond our windows. Like the burbling of a spring freshet, the flock's early-morning chatter was constant, an orchestra's tune-up before the symphony. There seemed to be no order to it; the big birds with their long necks were, I assumed, chattering back and forth—gossiping, perhaps, like old wives in the marketplace—reviewing the previous day's trip, discussing their flight plans for the day that dawned.

Then a sharper, more clarion call would sound, and soon I would hear the slap of broad wings on the water as the flock took wing with a rush of exertion, an audible struggle to get airborne. After the sibilant confusion of their takeoff, the geese would circle once or twice, and all chattering would stop. As the silence grew and I thought the geese had gone, the flight leader would call, this time with crystal clarity and authority. He left no doubt about who was in charge as the great birds took their places behind him, one after the other, in the V formation that so many artists have recorded on so much calendar art.

Then the geese would be gone, the sun would rise, and Chick and I would leave our warm beds, running down the hall and the stairs until we reached the warm kitchen with its radiant coal stove, dark wooden walls, and our grandfather's welcoming words. His was the brightest of spirits. For him, no day dawned that was not shining and charged with promise. A truly exceptional man. It is, now that I look back, that spirit of his that is woven deep in the tapestry the geese fashioned every spring.

In the late afternoon I walked to the dunes on the ocean side of that narrow neck of land, which pointed like a thin, gnarled finger toward the setting sun that tinted the Atlantic on one side and the pond on the other. Lying flat in the beach grass, still as the sand under me, I watched for geese on the far southern horizon. If the wind blew wet from the south or southwest, I knew there was a good chance the flocks would be riding it on their migration north to the subarctic tundra where they would nest and raise their young. I imagined they had traveled all day, perhaps even from the Chesapeake, with Georgica as their remembered destination, a safe place at the Atlantic's edge, a haven certified over the years as a rest stop they could fall into without anxiety.

And then I would hear the calling, this time quite different from the morning sounds. It would come on the wind, urgent, high-pitched, still melodious but somehow more piercing. These were weary birds, searching for sanctuary, yet ever alert to the unexpected. As I swept the skies, trying to locate the sound's source, I found a flock, each bird a thin line against the haze on the horizon. The twin tendrils of their wings moved in patient rhythm as they came closer, until I could distinguish the rounded bodies and their calling became clamorous because they could see the pond now, just beyond the dunes.

On my side, in the sand, I stayed still as a log, my head turned upward long before the geese reached the waves that broke there on the ocean's edge. I waited for the moment, hoping my good luck would bring the flight directly above me. And every now and then I was blessed. Immobile as I was, the geese may have seen me but were not alarmed. As is the case with most waterfowl, it is motion that would frighten them. As long as I did not move, I could, in their eyes, be that log I tried so hard to imitate.

My rewards were unforgettable. Already losing altitude in preparation for their landing on the pond, the geese would clear the dunes by just a few feet. There were times when I believed I could reach up and touch them as they whistled just above me. I could hear their wings creak and sigh, could see their white breasts, their buff torsos, and the white chin straps that highlighted their black heads. Often I could look straight into their brown eyes with those beady black pupils that seemed to stare directly into mine. Few people, I realize now, have ever been as close to so many wild birds in flight, close enough to see the minute striations of their feathers.

At night, after supper, after we slid into our chill beds, the same geese I wanted to touch chattered as they clustered together on the pond. Chick and I would fall asleep to the haunting melody of their wild, musical conversations.

Nearly a decade later, when I returned again to the same charmed house, geese became my prey. As a hunter of all waterfowl, I knew that killing a wild Canada goose was, in that part of the world, the ultimate act that would certify my skills with a shotgun. Yet for years that trophy eluded me. Six decades ago, there were not as many Canada geese as there are now, and the flocks on their annual migrations learned to be wary indeed during the fall hunting seasons.

In my years as a commercial fisherman, hauling seine nets along those same beaches of my boyhood, geese sometimes flew over our crew as we labored from dawn to dusk along the Atlantic's restless rim. In the course of fishing some twenty miles of beach, I learned a few things about the patterns Canada geese observed in their constant efforts to survive. I noticed, for example, that in late fall, flights of geese would wait until well after sunset (when gunning was illegal) to leave the relative safety of the open ocean, where they rafted in flocks during the day. As dusk edged toward darkness, those flocks would leave the open sea and ease into the potato fields just in back of the dunes, fields that in those days stretched along the oceanfront for miles and miles. Planted with winter wheat, they offered migrating waterfowl both rest and nourishment within sight of their oceanic refuge. And when fall rains flooded those fields, there was plenty of fresh water.

Sometimes there would be enough rain to create small potholes: ponds no larger than a tennis court, yet big enough to attract ducks and geese. One of these in the fields near Wainscott seemed especially favored. Sometimes after fishing, as the sky darkened, I waited with my shotgun at that nameless pothole's edge, facing west so I could see a bird's outline against the twilight sky. Even though the remaining light was little more than a pale, luminous strip just above the horizon, it was enough to silhouette a duck's dark shape as it drifted in for a landing. That was all I needed to be able to aim and shoot, and it was the method I used most often when I wanted to bring a wild duck home for the dinner table. I knew it was illegal, but it was also most effective, and the spot was so remote that I never worried about being apprehended. Indeed, I felt so confident about my secret pothole, I promised my bride I'd bring home a Thanksgiving goose.

I began waiting in the field each evening, waiting for that goose. It came out of a cloudy November sky. I fired, and the sound of a splash was loud, final. There on the silvery surface lay my Thanksgiving goose, its wings extended, its neck and head underwater.

Wading into the pothole, I lifted the great bird high; it was a large goose, better than ten pounds. I was so proud. But only for that instant. As I turned back toward the shore, a figure rose from the field: looming, broad-shouldered, stolid, and authoritarian. It was Nick Catalina, Suffolk County's game warden. He had been waiting for me, had been told by someone who had heard my shotgun booming on other evenings that somebody was dusking there in the Wainscott field.

He took my goose and my hunting license and had me follow him to his office in Bridgehampton, where he filled out papers that required me to pay a $200 fine and forfeit my right to hunt for a full year. And he kept the goose. For me that was the most painful of my punishments, although the $200 came in a close second. In those days, that was a considerable sum, especially for a commercial fisherman.

Over the next several decades of my gunning years, I killed more geese, some over decoys set out in fields very close to that Wainscott pothole. But I shot no more illegally; and, as I passed middle age, I quit killing completely.

But Canada geese were never out of my life. Their comings and goings left their stitches in the complex embroidery of my erratic career; it seemed that no matter where I lived or what I did for a living, the geese would be there. And not merely in the background. Their presence, or their arrival, was always duly noted as a strong signal of reassurance, a kind of guarantee that this symbol of natural integrity was still with us. Hearing that unmistakable call assured me that this most visible and audible certification of the wild still prevailed.

When we first moved to the Maine coast region that would become my lifetime home, our farmhouse on Merrymeeting Bay included a few acres of fields worked by a truck farmer who raised corn, parsnips, and carrots. Each March, just as they had during those grade-school years of my anxious boyhood, great flocks of geese would sweep by, circle, and land in the open spaces just beyond our barn. At night, under the blankets, I could hear their sweet chattering and be swept back over thirty years to those weekends at our grandparents' when Chick lay in the bed next to mine, both of us awed by the wildness of the sounds from the pond just beyond our windows

And on the day-by-day calendar I have kept so diligently for almost twenty years I have duly noted the arrival of the first Canada goose to signal the eventual end of Maine's implacable winters. At least that's how it used to be. Now I learn that I have lived long enough to witness a remarkable change in the ageless (well, once thought to be ageless) migratory patterns of the Canada goose. According to highly qualified observers of the U.S. Fish & Wildlife Service, some 700,000 of the estimated 1.2 million Atlantic Canada geese no longer migrate. After a millennia of travel in tune with the four seasons, the birds now stay where they are throughout the year. They have become, in Fish & Wildlife terminology, sedentary.

How the mighty have fallen. And how dismal, in the process, has their once proud reputation become. Just ask some of the golfers and golf-course caretakers in Connecticut, or New Jersey or almost anywhere on Long Island. Their stories of how vast flocks of Canada geese have all but ruined expensive fairways and velvet putting greens should bring tears to the eyes of anyone who has ever steered a golf cart.

Every deterrent under the sun has been tested in the ongoing battle against the flocks, which consume just about any grass or grain that's grown. They graze like sheep, and their black bills— serrated and curved like a cutting tool—can clip grass closer than any sheep, and in remarkable amounts. A young Canada gosling, for example, will gain twenty-four times its birth weight in eight weeks. A newborn seven-pound human boy or girl, growing at the same speed, would tip the scales at 168 two months later.

And once the nutrients are removed from the roughage swallowed with such unflagging appetites, Canadas are equally prolific with the waste that remains. More than one golfer has had to pick up his ball because it was impossible to find any dependable footing on the layers of fresh goose doo-doo coating the fairways.

Here in Maine, the problems with sedentary geese have yet to reach critical mass. But there is enough of a permanent population to dispel all the romance I once attached to seeing or hearing that first migratory goose of March. According to Brad Allen of Maine's Department of Inland Fisheries and Wildlife, the state's sedentary geese are adapting well to their new, non-migratory life.

"Thanks to the comparatively mild winters we've enjoyed for the past several years," he reports, "we have counted up to 2,000 wintering geese. There's a large flock that hangs out on the golf course at the Samoset resort [in Rockport] and another that likes Mackworth Island just east of Portland. And they're doing very well. Four years ago, the Arctic migratory flock was badly hurt by a June snowstorm. Their entire nesting season was wiped out. Meanwhile, the Maine birds have had almost ideal nesting conditions. There's almost no mortality, very few predators. With an average of five eggs to a clutch and as many as 500 nesting pairs, exponentially speaking it won't be long before Maine's population of sedentary geese begins to add up.

"So," concludes Allen, "we're looking at a whole new can of worms."

Or a surfeit of geese.

I got a hint of what that might be like on a recent trip to New Jersey. Traveling the highway from Newark to Princeton is a trip through one of the manufacturing centers of the northeast. It is not a journey for those who yearn for open spaces, broad vistas, and natural presences. And yet, there the geese were, crowding drainage ponds in the shadow of a plastics-molding plant, picking at grass on the well tended front lawn of a computer-chip producer, and even lined up on the tattered turf of the median strip that divides a highway churning with tractor trailers and the delivery trucks of a thousand manufacturers.

Stalled there in the endless traffic, I looked out my window directly into the eyes of a median-browsing Canada goose. I was close enough to see the striations of its creamy breast feathers, a sight that took me back to those boyhood adventures on the dunes when I lay still as a log and could hear the great goose wings creak as the birds flew just above me, the wonder of their wildness almost close enough to touch.

Even though there seemed little to connect those birds of the median strip with the icons of my youth, there was, nevertheless, enough. Looking out that car window, I could hear the wild sounds of my past, our past, mine and the bird's, linked forever by the quintessential mystery of that call of the Canada, as haunting a sound as there is in all of nature.

American Crow

(Corvus brachyrhynchos)

Almost every afternoon now I walk to the river and back along the gravel road that runs by the side of our home. It's only a quarter-mile or so from our barn to the tall stand of mature white pine that rises green between the house and the Androscoggin. Through the woods there's a narrow path that ends where the cattails and marsh grass slope to the water's edge and to a small bump of muddy beach where I stand and watch the river glide by. Along this stretch, the Androscoggin is placid; sometimes, when it hasn't rained for a long while, the current sags so that it's all but invisible.

But if I look upriver I see nothing but the Androscoggin, sunsplashed and bright, and the tree-covered banks that rise on both sides into a pair of sloping hills held there by oaks, hemlock, pine, maple, ash, birch, and patches of alder. That's all I can see: trees, sky, clouds, and the river. It's about the same as what I might have seen had I stood in this spot a thousand or maybe two thousand years ago, although the woods might have been quite different then. I'm sure they've been cut over several times during the millennia. But the idea that I can stand here a few miles from downtown and look out over such a pure and unblemished natural vista buzzes me with tremors of wonder and gratitude every single time.

As I stood there the other evening restoring my soul, a lone crow flew over from behind me, high, moving lazily, crossing the

river. Another followed, then a third, this one a bit lower, his totally black presence dramatically singular against white clouds and that brilliant blue sky.

As I have done throughout my life almost every time I meet a crow on the wing, I called to that bird. It's become second nature for me. Looking directly at the crow above, I let loose with what has been a long-practiced imitation of how a crow shouts when it wants to tell its associates to, "Come see what I've found." I am, as every member of our family will tell you with real conviction, totally tone deaf. But somehow I have managed over more than a half-century of practice to hit precisely the right notes when it comes to calling crows. Like the sound of a slide trombone, it's all but impossible to translate to the written word. *Caaw! . . . Caaw! . . . Caaw!* with a kind of dragged out, but excited, final note looks silly in print. But if you could hear me at my best, you would be quite convinced a crow was nearby.

As I called to that Androscoggin bird, it stayed on course across the river, never even turned its head for a look around. I must have lost my crow voice, I told myself. But that never stopped me from continuing my calling.

And when it reached the opposite bank and appeared to be heading for the woods across the river, that crow pivoted, turned 180 degrees, and headed straight toward me, calling as it came. I stood still, hoping my tan shirt and pants were blending with the marsh grass and the brush at my back. Absolute paralysis, no movement of any sort, not even the blink of an eye: that's the first imperative if you want birds to approach you. All birds are wary of movement, but most birds, the crow included, are not alarmed by a motionless object, even if it's tall, two-legged, and wearing a hat.

As that crow came closer, I could see three more birds starting to set the same course as they gained altitude above the opposite riverbank, then turned my way, accelerating with rapid wingbeats. If there was anything to be seen, those crows were determined not to miss out. That's the way of crows: if one of them makes a discovery, even if it's a discouraging one like a great-horned owl, every other crow in the neighborhood will do its damnedest to get into the act.

In moments, four crows were above me, circling, calling, talking to each other, questioning, trying to locate the bird that had sent them the "Hey, come see what I've got" signal.

When I took off my cap and waved it at them, those crows did a double-take, then hustled off, irritated at being fooled, and somewhat alarmed at being too close to a human being. For me, the moment was eminently satisfactory, one to be remembered. Of each of the several ways I've learned to make close contact with natural presences, calling crows is one of the best. I am, after all, communicating with a wild creature in a very direct and quantifiable way: I talk with crows and they, in turn, not only talk with me but approach me directly to do so. Those same sons and daughters and grandsons who laugh whenever I sing(?) "Smoke Gets In Your Eyes" are invariably properly impressed when they watch me call crows. I hope they are impressed enough to begin to try it on their own; the rewards are far more complex than most, and yet they are there for anyone who wants to make the effort.

I began learning more than fifty years ago, when crows were legally shot and killed every month of the year. All the rod-and-gun magazines published articles about crow shooting, stories that detailed the big, black bird's predations: how it killed fledgling songbirds in their nests, stole all manner of birds' eggs, and ate the farmer's hard-won ears of corn. The crow's most heinous offense, cried the outdoor writers, was destroying entire broods of infant waterfowl in their nests, wild ducklings and goslings that should have survived to become targets for the nation's duck and goose hunters, those "sportsmen" who were the rightful beneficiaries of all that nature creates.

Crow shoots in places like Ohio and Missouri became feature articles in *Field & Stream,* along with photographs of small hills of dead crows, or barrels overflowing with black feathers all awry. Chick and I read those magazines; we learned about crow decoys and crow calls; and, most important, we understood crow shooting to be a virtuous act, executed in the name of conservation and the greater protection of "good" birds and "useful" wildlife.

We bought a P. S. Olt crow call at Robertson & Zenger, the

Main Street hunting and fishing store, and we fashioned silhouette crow decoys from stiff, black roofing paper. This we cut to a crow's shape (outlined by Chick, the artist) and stapled to double thickness around a single, pointed dowel that could be stuck in the ground.

We'd set out a dozen of those decoys at the edge of a cornfield and hunker down in the brush with our shotguns while I began blowing on the P. S. Olt, a cylinder of black Bakelite, no longer than a cigarette, fitted with a reed set to vibrate at a crow's cawing pitch. I found it worked best if I hummed into it as I blew, and I learned the three-or-four-*caaw* call that brought crows circling over our heads.

Often those birds would dispatch a single scout to check out my calling. That scout never uttered a sound; many times we never even saw it as it glided overhead on silent wings. And if we did spot it, that crow was out of range before we could swing our shotguns on target. We developed respect for the crow's intelligent wariness and we got better at deception. There were times when we had crows circling our decoys, cawing, apparently unalarmed by our presence. Then we'd shoot down three or four, and tell ourselves what good crow hunters we were.

We never knew what to do with our crow carcasses, so we brought them home in a burlap bag and dumped them in the garbage. Even then, I'm certain, in spite of the endless crow-hunting propaganda we'd absorbed throughout our impressionable adolescence, both of us felt tremors of guilt when we had to carry out that inevitable job of dead crow disposal.

But although an accumulation of those moments may have dampened our crow-shooting ardor, we never quite stopped. Crows became targets of opportunity—every possible opportunity. Once, driving along the Montauk Highway on our way to hunt ducks in Gardiners Bay, I sat in the back seat of an open convertible with a 12-gauge pump gun held upright between my knees. Just west of Napeague, a line of crows flew alongside the car for a few moments. I stood, braced myself against the seat back, picked up the shotgun, dropped a shell in the chamber, swung on a crow flying parallel to us, fired, and dropped it cleanly into the beach grass and bayberry shrubs. The car never slowed. It was quite a shot. After fifty-six years, I can still see it all happening, in detail.

A year or so later, I was at the U.S. Army Air Corps aerial gunnery training center in Kingman, Arizona. As future combat flyers, we had to learn how to shoot at an attacking aircraft with machine guns and 20-millimeter cannons aboard our moving planes. It was, our gunnery trainers told us, a different sort of shooting that required a special sort of aiming. For practice, that first week at Kingman, we climbed in the back of open Army trucks, where we stood with our shotguns as the trucks drove fairly fast around a track. As we drove, clay targets were launched unexpectedly from a series of well camouflaged locations. Those targets flew by just like that crow at Napeague; I broke almost all of them on our first circuit, which earned me a "well done" from our training officer. Perhaps that's the fundamental reason I've always remembered that Napeague crow.

Not long after gunnery training, I was flying in a real war where real bullets and antiaircraft shells were aimed at our aircraft every time we flew. I saw a good many planes like ours get shot down, or explode in midair. A lot of good men I knew lost their lives or their limbs. By the time the war ended and I returned home in good shape, I'd changed. I didn't quit bird hunting, not then, but I never killed another crow. Something about killing them just for killing's sake no longer seemed justifiable to me. These are complex decisions; many influences (some quite beyond our knowing) are at work, and simple explanations are not forthcoming. If they are, they should be suspect.

But, ironically, crows and I became close friends during my crow-shooting years. Unless I'd been a serious ornithologist, and at that age I was serious about very little, there is no way except as my quarry that I would have learned so much about those rascally black birds. And I most assuredly would never have learned how to converse with them. Hunting, in spite of its fervent detractors, is not entirely without its redemption. Crows and I are a fine example. Because, as its hunter, I spent so much time studying crow habits and habitats, I learned that this is a remarkable bird: intelligent, curious, and resourceful. It is a caring parent and a creature with a full range of social behaviors, including a finely sophisticated sense of humor and a kind of elitism that has always appealed to me.

Yes, it's true that crows are bandits. They steal, they gang up on smaller birds, they harass their competitors, and they can drive a full-grown house cat into hiding. They are raucous, gossipy, possessive, and comic—traits that are all too human. Crows are also garrulous; they talk all the time, even when they don't need to. Which, in my case, is a blessing, for now that I know something of their language, I can talk to crows whenever our paths cross. During the past half-century they have crossed many more times than you might imagine.

In the northeastern United States, the American crow is ubiquitous and has adapted to all environments. Nothing humans do to alter those environments seems to have much effect on the crow; however traumatic the changes, this remarkable bird finds their benefits, no matter how marginal.

Tens of thousands of square miles of woods and fields have been obliterated to make room for the turnpikes and highways that wind around the lower forty-eight states like jungle vines. These masses of concrete, most of us would assume, are surely the antithesis of nature, sterile habitats suitable for all manner of vehicles, but little else. Yet the crows are there, alongside Interstate 95, on the Merritt Parkway median, and the Pennsylvania Turnpike. On any give day as you travel our superhighways, you can look out your driver's-side window and see a crow. From the moment the first highway was built, crows discovered roadkill. All manner of quadrupeds—rabbits, porcupines, groundhogs, squirrels, skunks, cats, dogs, deer, and more—are struck down by vehicles every night and day, and crows are bold enough to make meals of each one.

Bold enough and smart enough. Crows have deciphered the physics of vehicles traveling seventy miles per hour and faster. The birds know just how close to the median a tractor-trailer will veer and they've learned that vehicles in the breakdown lane travel slowly enough to be avoided. Like most birds, crows are carnivores, flesh eaters that can make a meal of a flattened rabbit as readily as they can bolt down a newly hatched swarm of grasshoppers or the corn kernels left in the fields by mechanical harvesters. These birds are the champion opportunists of the winged world and have adapted so cleverly to the often destructive march of human progress that there are now more crows than ever among us.

Which is why I'm grateful that as a young man I learned something of their language and their behavior. That knowledge has allowed me to talk with crows, to play games with them, and , every now and then, to play harmless tricks on them. Although often, I've discovered, I turn out to be the one who's been tricked. For crows, as you'll soon learn if you take up with them, are smarter than most birds . . . way smarter.

BLUE-WINGED TEAL
(Anas discors)

∽

It was an afternoon in early September almost forty years ago when I first stood on the shores of Merrymeeting Bay, one of the great waterfowl gathering grounds on the East Coast. That's when I had my first proper introduction to blue-winged teal. I had seen the bird before, but from a distance and only very occasionally. But there on Merrymeeting's shores I was granted an exhibition of grace and splendor. At the time, of course, I had no way of knowing that this lovely and diminutive bird would do for my duck hunting what the Napeague crow had done for my shooting. On that luminous September afternoon, this critical moment was far in my future.

I'd traveled to Bowdoinham with a real estate agent to see a place he had advertised. It was a farmhouse with an attached barn, the way they are in Maine, on five acres that fronted the bay. The house, like so many in the state's rural communities, was just a few feet off the road; that's so a minimal amount of snow would have to be plowed. But a path went through the field to the shores of Merrymeeting, and there at the water's edge under a large, old oak was a small log cabin. It looked like something from the time of Daniel Boone and when I saw it, I walked right past the main house toward the bay.

When I reached the bank that sloped down to the cattails and bulrushes where the bay lapped at the sandy shore, at least thirty

teal flushed from a pothole twenty feet or so offshore; that was more blue-wings than I'd seen in my duck-hunting life.

I was mesmerized. Teal are among the swiftest of all waterfowl and are surely the most graceful and elusive flyers. They bank, turn, spin, soar, glide, and flash past at sixty miles per hour or better, as those lovely powder-blue wing patches dance ever so lightly on the air. I sat down in the reeds and stayed motionless for five minutes; the blue-wings returned, circling, darting past not ten feet from me. I could see their eyes clearly, hear the rush of crisp September air through their feathers along with the delicate peeping of the drakes as they called to each other like children in an enchanted forest.

"I'll take it," I told the broker when I finally walked back to the main house.

"But don't you want to see the inside?"

"No thanks. I've seen more than enough to convince me this is the right place for us."

I'm sure that broker hasn't made many quicker or easier sales. But we paid no penalties for my enthusiasm; the house was a fine one, and the barn was in good shape. Best of all, Linwood Rideout and his wife, the sellers, lived just a short ways down the road in a new home Linwood had built. They became fine friends. Linwood is one of the old-time Merrymeeting Bay duck-hunting guides and is generous with his time and information. Because of him, I knew a great deal about the bay and its wild birds before I ever hunted them.

Most of the first thirty days we lived in that house were teal-watching days for me. Even with our unpacking chores and my new job as a newspaper editor in neighboring Brunswick, I found many hours when I could sit quietly in the bulrushes and watch blue wings as they fluttered, dipped, and soared over the marshes that were now in our front yard. The presence of those teal was, for me, a gift that far exceeded all my dreams and expectations.

In mid-October when the first half of the two-part hunting season began, my times with teal were ended for the year. The rumbling roar of a hundred guns on opening day was the signal for all the bay's waterfowl to be on the alert, to clear out, if possible, before dawn and to return after sunset when the shooting stopped. But not every bird behaved with such caution—especially in the first days of the season, when blue-wings were among the most foolish. I shot one or two on opening day, and our part Labrador retriever, part English setter (named Teal long before we came to Merrymeeting) found another half-dozen cripples in the rushes and brush. These he proudly brought back to me, holding them ever so delicately in his soft mouth.

Fattened in preparation for their southward migration, those teal were—without a doubt—the finest wild ducks I ever had for dinner. Feeding on Merrymeeting's wild rice had given them more than fine, plump breasts; it had blessed them with a delicate, nutty flavor that set my taste buds soaring. During each of the duck-hunting years that followed, I treasured no reward as much as the taste of those early season blue-winged teal.

But in spite of such delicious benefits, my duck hunting ardor cooled over the years, a change of life difficult for me to comprehend. I wondered what had become of the guy who could never sleep before a day of duck hunting, that young fellow who once sat for hours in a freezing rain hoping for a single shot, who swam alone into the chill surf of an October Atlantic to retrieve a fallen scoter or drove all night through the snow for a chance at another day on the marshes. What had become of him, especially now that he lived right on top of some of the finest duck hunting in the nation? I wasn't sure. All I knew was that what had once been pure obsession had become a diversion I could take or leave alone. More and more frequently, I found, I left it alone.

I was getting older. That's one of the changes. But it wasn't the only one. I was also having serious doubts about whether I should kill anything, ever. That was a much more serious, and troubling, development. After all, during my adolescence and young manhood, guns and hunting—along with fishing—had been among the greatest joys of my life. Better than sex, as I have said so frequently.

In a kind of homage to the many days of duck hunting I had

enjoyed, I kept at it, but in a much more ceremonial fashion. On the season's opening day I made the effort to be out on the Merrymeeting marshes, and I shot over decoys one or two days after that. A dozen years went by, years of change for me and my family. We moved to Brunswick, closer to my job and the children's schools, but ducks and geese were still part of my awareness each day. I watched for their return flights in the spring, listened for their calling across the bays every frosty October evening. And killed fewer and fewer of them.

During that twelfth autumn, my brother Chick called from his home in Connecticut. "How about duck shooting," he said, "like we used to?" It was a sweet and sentimental try at recapturing those long-ago teenage years when we shivered, wet and wretched, in a November nor'easter, hunched in the brush by some nameless pothole, hoping for a wild duck. We wanted just one, any one, any species, to come whistling in, wings spread, the way they did in all those dozens of waterfowling books and magazines we read in those superbly innocent times of our lives.

Of course, I said yes. I would have said yes to any chance to spend time with Chick. We were, he and I, alone together during much of our boyhood; we roomed together when we were sent off to boarding school at ages ten and eleven. As the youngest boarders, we needed each other's presence and support. So, our bonds reached far back.

Having arrived in time for dinner on a chill October evening, Chick stayed up later than he should have talking with Jean and me, and neither of us got much sleep. We got up at five, grabbed a cup of coffee and some toast, and left the house in the dark. Patches of ground fog curled across the road during our drive to a friend's place on Merrymeeting's shores; he had agreed to lend us a gunning float, and I had a borrowed five-horse outboard in the car.

The fog, which had been patchy inland, became a cottony blanket spread across the entire bay. At first light, it was still so thick we couldn't see much beyond our own bow, but we expected it to burn off once the sun eased far enough above the horizon to generate some heat. Feeling our way along the edge of the marsh, we anchored somewhere near a spot I'd shot over the year before. I'd dropped seven black-duck decoys a short way offshore, and by the time we were settled, hunkered down in the cramped gunning float, the fog was so dense we could hardly see our rig.

Every now and then we could hear the unique and thrilling whistle and rush of a wild duck's wings in free flight. And once in a while the almost comic, raucous call of a black-duck hen would sound loud in our ears, amplified by the fog, which persisted in making our atmosphere more water than air.

So we knew there were ducks in our vicinity, even though we had yet to see a single one.

As the chill of the late October's near-freezing morning worked its way past our thermal long underwear and into our bones, we traded oblique suggestions of surrender to the fog, a capitulation that would see us headed home without having fired a shot. But each time, we told each other we'd give it another half-hour. And at last the fog began to lose its grip. Not totally, but enough so our decoys showed up and our visibility improved from zero to fifty yards. By then, we'd been sitting hunched over in the wet cold for almost two hours.

Which was when the blue-winged teal came fluttering, hurtling out of the mist, parallel to our float from my left.

Chick was on my right, so technically the shot was mine. I raised my long-barreled, twelve-gauge pump and tried to swing far enough in front of that sixty-mile-an-hour target.

As I did, Chick suddenly stood up, his knees all but paralyzed by his two hours of immobility. He tipped forward a bit as I pulled the trigger, just as I reached the limit of my cramped swing.

Bang! How shattering the explosion sounded. It startled both of us, and Chick was so shaken he dropped his double-barreled shotgun in the bay. Because I had swung so far, and because he had stood up without warning me, I came with an inch or two of shooting my brother, the man I loved more than any other. At that close range, any wound would have killed him.

Both of us paled, close to shock.

"Jesus, John," Chick said, "I can't go back without that gun."

Nothing about how close I'd come to killing him, just utter desperation about recovering the shotgun my reckless act had made him drop.

"That's John Hettinger's Parker," he said. "It's engraved and everything." Chick began taking off his outer layer of clothes, stripping down to his longies. I could understand why. Even in those days, a premium-grade Parker fetched more than ten thousand dollars.

Over the side he went, gasping at the cold. Taking a breath, he went under, his stockinged feet kicking on the surface. Up he came with a *woosh*, but no Parker. Back down, back up. "I felt it," he yelled and went under again. This time he surfaced with the gun held high.

He started shivering as soon as he crawled into the boat. I paddled out, grabbed the decoys, started the cranky outboard, and headed for the dock at top speed, worried about the possibility of hypothermia.

On the way in, through fog patches that still held their places, the boat ran over a mostly submerged length of pulpwood. When the four-foot log hit the outboard's shaft, it shoved the outboard upwards with enough force to knock the borrowed motor right off the stern. It sank, bubbling, in the murky water.

It was my turn go overboard.

When I finally recovered the outboard, it was clotted with Merrymeeting Bay mud and wrapped in eelgrass. I plunked it on the stern and paddled the rest of the way to the dock. When we got there a half-hour later, both of us were shivering uncontrollably. Not even the drive home with the car's heater on full tilt did much to warm us.

That had to wait until we reached the indoors, got out of our wet clothes, and into hot showers. Then, sitting at our kitchen table with steaming cups of coffee in our hands and some of Jean's beef stew on our plates, we began to feel human.

Jean laughed and said we made a fine pair of duck hunters. "The ducks almost got you both," she said, and in a way she was right, as usual.

"I think maybe we're getting too old for this," I said.

Chick looked back at me from across the table. "I think you may be right," he said, shaking his head at the wondrous ineptitude of our mishaps and near tragedy.

That was, in fact, the last time I ever went duck shooting. And the last time I ever fired a shotgun at any bird I meant to kill. After more than a quarter-century, my gunning days were over. I don't regret a single one of them, just as I have never regretted my decision to quit.

The blue-winged teal that caused so much physical and emotional turmoil, by the way, kept right on flying. I missed it, cleanly.

I see it still, however, and will, I suppose, for all of my years. And, luckily for me, a few teal stop over each mid-September on the reach of the Androscoggin River just a short ways from our home. If I walk quietly enough through the woods, I can stand there on the river's edge behind the cattails and watch these delightful ducks swimming and feeding in the shallows. And if I'm very lucky, one or two will fly by. How swift, how graceful they are, dipping and darting, the late afternoon sun catching that sky-blue patch on their wings, the tremulous peeping of their calling as soft as the river's ripple.

HERRING GULL
(Larus argentatus)

Ajll birds are opportunists. It's essential to their survival in an unforgiving environment. Nature offers no handouts; there is no welfare for the disadvantaged. Every bird lives by its food-finding skills and every bird is quick to capitalize on any newly discovered supply. But in my experience, no bird I have met is more of an opportunist than the herring gull. Which must account for the fact that as the human population in the northeastern United States has grown and, for the most part, prospered, so too has the herring gull.

These large white birds with the gray wings, chrome-yellow bills, and cold, pale-yellow eyes are ubiquitous along Maine's coast, where I have seen them almost every day of each of the several decades I have shared that shoreline with them. I meet them whenever I set sail in any sort of watercraft. Most often, those gulls I greet at sea are following a lobster boat, circling her like a tethered white whirlwind, around and around, screaming in their high-pitched, querulous tones, diving on any bait scraps or hapless crabs tossed from the lobsterman's traps.

The same screaming pursues gillnetters, longliners, or draggers as their crews dress out the catch, tossing a multihued stream of fish guts, heads, and gill rakers overboard, where they thread astern for a half-mile or more, an offal signature that certifies the day's hard labor.

Herring gulls trail those fishing boats like paid mourners behind a hearse, wailing, shrieking and often quarreling over a strand of haddock intestine as if it were the only scrap on a sea that's littered with them. But as noisy, noisome, and ill-mannered as they may be, these herring gulls are doing a job, and a good one. Like the Serengeti vultures, which polish off (literally) the carcasses left by lions, herring gulls are the carrion sweepers of the seas.

And working fishermen are not their only source of supply. Bluefish, those tigers of the open oceans, are among the most predatory hunters of the inshore Atlantic, often killing tons of herring, butterfish, or menhaden when their appetites could have been sated with just a few hundred pounds. The leftovers are a bonus the herring gull has learned to love. Which is why the sight of one of these feathered whirlwinds over open water is a signal every angler recognizes and welcomes. Let just one bluefish break the surface with a single, foamy splash and within moments fifty gulls will join him, tracking the school from above, marking it with a swirling, screaming cluster of large white birds visible a half-mile off. Finding surface-feeding fish—striped bass, tuna, bonito, albacore, and weakfish, as well as predatory blues—is one of the things herring gulls do best.

Of their many scavenger roles, this is the one that generates the most favorable image. If the herring gull restricted its diet to commercial fishery castoffs and the acres of shredded bait fish left in the wake of feeding schools of blues, its image would be secure and respected. But being the talented and diligent opportunist that it is, this bird sullies its reputation with frequent forays to strip-mall parking lots, municipal garbage dumps, marinas where recreational fish catches are cleaned, fast-food emporiums, plowed fields, outdoor restaurants (especially those on the waterfront), inner city parks, trout hatcheries, zoos, yacht basins, ferryboats, baseball stadiums, canneries, racetracks, poultry farms, sidewalk cafes, mobile-home parks, campsites, and the polished granite steps of county courthouses, where legal secretaries sit in brilliant lunch-time sunshine to nibble on tacos or slices of pepperoni pizza.

These kind-hearted souls toss the last of their crusts to a waiting herring gull. As a result of what is, in fact, a free lunch, and because herring gulls are such fast learners when it comes to new nourishment opportunities, there now are, I'm certain, more gulls finding a living off the water than on it. No longer a target of feather hunters, protected by federal laws, and freed from the predations of humans, who once gathered protein-rich gull eggs by the tens of thousands from the bird's island rookeries, herring gulls have enjoyed a quarter-century population explosion.

This growth has, in some places, reached the crisis stage, prompted primarily by the white splash of herring-gull droppings across the hoods of costly automobiles, the courthouse roof, park benches, and—every now and then—the padded shoulder of a banker's thousand-dollar suit. No such prominent citizen reacts with equanimity when zapped with gull shit as he strolls the town common, where gulls gather in the spring to greet the freshly painted hot-dog wagons and celebrate the end of a long New England winter.

Strutting across the common with more assurance than any banker, the herring gull throws back his head; extends his neck; opens wide that hooked yellow bill; and cuts loose with a bugling, shrill, clarion territorial cry that has become one of the most commanding natural sounds heard in any town or city. It is a cry that echoes from a hundred television commercials, that's mixed in the theme music for a score of movies, and that is romanticized as a background for a dozen popular love songs that have been on the charts for decades. Whenever any writer, promoter, lyricist, or script fixer wants to evoke the ineffable purity of the waterfront, the briny tang of salt air, it is the herring gull's bodacious cry that's chosen. Properly orchestrated, this bird sound can be magic. After a few notes, we forget every depredation the herring gull hath wrought. All malice vanishes. Only romance remains.

Which is very lucky for the herring gull. A while back, enough thousand-dollar suits had been soiled in Maine to spark an anti-gull movement with sufficient momentum to send properly licensed, government-approved gull killers off to several of the most popular island rookeries along the coast. Wielding long-needled hypodermic syringes loaded with poison, the gull-control squads spent weeks injecting gull eggs in their nests, not only killing the embryos within, but deceiving the parents into incubating and caring for eggs that would never hatch.

But the gulls were not gulled. Messages beyond our ken informed them of the internal slaughter of the unborn innocents. The herring gulls responded by breeding over and over again until they finally created eggs that hatched. By then, the gull-control plan, which looked fine in theory, had proven inefficient in practice.

Which is OK with me. While I don't have much genuine affection for herring gulls (it's difficult to love a bird that craps on your boat), I respect them for their bravado and for the essence of the sea that's captured in their cry. And, now that I think of it, I've come close to loving them for the many times they have found fish for me, signaling me from across the water, pointing with the tip of their feathery, whirling funnel at a school of feeding stripers I might never otherwise have found.

It's also difficult to dislike a bird you've known all your life. As an infant I spent my very first summer within window-rattling distance of the open Atlantic's breaking surf, so herring gulls must have been among the very first birds I met. And I can remember, when I grew old enough to walk on my own, coming up over the crest of the dunes along that ocean beach and seeing small feathered assemblies at the sea's foaming edge. There herring gulls gathered like farmers on the steps of a general store discussing the weather.

Later in life, when I had a job in Manhattan (I hesitate to claim I was "working"), I learned that if I kept my eyes on the sky, I would soon spot a herring gull. They joined me at baseball games at the Polo Grounds and Yankee Stadium, hovered above the reservoir in Central Park, and patrolled the East River with the diligence of those who understood that the much abused waterway could cough up refuse more exotic than a gull was likely to find anywhere else on the coast.

And the very first day I set foot in Portland, Maine, all those long years ago, I heard the shrill proclamation of a herring gull as it circled above City Hall's gilded dome, surveying the building's steps and benches for edible discards: a hot-dog stub here, a fragment of cupcake there. The moment that unique screech drew its keen blade across my consciousness, I knew Portland would always hold a high place in my affections.

Further verification followed when the city adopted the herring gull as one of its directional icons. "Follow the gull" said the signposts pointing to places where visitors would be courteously relieved of their spending money.

After all these years, the herring gulls are still with me. Our home on the Androscoggin is several miles from the coast and another few miles from the town dump. As the gull flies, we are a mid-way checkpoint. Each morning as I shave and glance out the window, I see my old buddy, the herring gull, making its patient way north. Neither snow, sleet, wind, or even an abundance of fresh fish elsewhere in Casco Bay can dissuade these dogged scavengers from their mission. And in the evening when I step outdoors, my day's work done, those same gulls are flapping south, headed for the offshore island that is their guano-bleached rookery and roost.

Every now and then I tell Jean to look. "There go the gulls," I say, "on their way home from work. When they get there, their wives will ask, 'Another tough day at the dump, dear?'"

COMMON TERN
(Sterna hirundo)

✦

A s the seasons come and go, I watch for the arrivals and departures of many birds. It is their presence that verifies a spring, or their absence that certifies winter. But of all these many comings and goings, none is more carefully observed than the common tern's return sometime during the middle of May. And I make an extra effort not to miss it. I'll take a drive to Simpson's Point, park the car, and walk to the water's edge, where I can scan twenty or thirty square miles of Middle Bay.

Beyond the bay, out there to the south, the Atlantic begins; I can see it on the horizon. It is from out there somewhere in that blue infinity that the terns will come like fragile white arrows loosed from an unseen bow. They will fly in with the flooding tide, pursuing the tiny silver fish that are their sustenance. Diving like darters, the terns mark their hunt with blossoms of white water no larger than a daisy. If I listen carefully, I can hear their high-pitched calling, one telling the other about fish it has found, or perhaps merely expressing its exuberance at being alive. They are such excitable, vital creatures, these small, streamlined, all-but-weightless birds that seem to live each day at the summit of their considerable energies.

Sighting that first mid-May arrival here in Maine reassures me that our long winter and reluctant spring have truly run their course. Now that the terns are back, I tell myself, we can lay claim to summer with real confidence. For it is summer that the terns

bring with them, that and the echoes of my past sounding in their screams.

Off the north end of Gardiners Island, at the end of a thin and wavering finger of sand that's flooded at high tide, are the ruins of a fort. Called the "Old Fort" or simply "The Ruins," they're what's left of the stone walls of an eighteenth-century fort built, like so many military projects, for contingencies that never materialized. And because it is a lonely and deserted place charged with mystery, it has always been a fine destination for boys in search of adventure.

Which is why a group of us set sail for the Old Fort from Devon back there in those pre-war days of such awesome innocence. We would, we told our parents, be camping there for the night.

Skinny, plagued by the strains of adolescence, yet unwilling to admit to any frailty, we considered sleeping under the sky a kind of proof of our independence and virility, if, indeed, a fourteen year old can possess those virtues.

We sailed out in a pair of comfortable catboats on a late June afternoon, allowing plenty of time to prepare for our campfire and the weenie roast to come. We carried enough provisions ashore to sustain a military platoon for a week.

But we encountered stiff resistance the moment we entered what had been the old fort's inner courtyard, the spot we had chosen to make camp. Screaming with grinding, high-pitched cries— almost a wail—dozens of nesting terns swooped and dove at us, circling relentlessly, then diving straight at the top of our heads. We had to duck; those birds appeared to have every intention of driving their sharp, black-tipped, orange bills through our scalps or, worse yet, into our very eyes.

At first, we had no idea why these birds were behaving so violently. None of us had yet spent much time, if any, exploring details of the natural world around us. But when at last we became aware of the tern nests and their tiny, spotted, downy occupants, we understood. The birds we had first assumed were driven by an insane and inexplicable outrage were protecting their young, those golf-ball-sized bits of fluff scattered in shallow depressions here and there amid the old fort's sandstone rubble.

We surrendered and withdrew, packing out all that we had brought inside those tumbled walls. We moved to the farthest point from the fort, an open, sandy spit quite without shelter of any sort. There we built our driftwood fire, warmed our hot dogs, and spent the evening huddled against the chill southwest wind, trying our best to sleep in the dank sand. All these years later, I would be willing to swear that I never put together two fifteen-minute stretches of real sleep during that wretched June night. Never was any group of adventurers happier to see that early dawn. As soon as there was light enough, we broke camp and began our homeward sail, leaving that old fort to the terns, which had gotten there first and knew how to defend the place they called home.

Ten years later, after taking part in a real war, I returned to Gardiners Bay as a fisherman, and my feelings for the tern converted from fear to affection, from annoyance to great respect. And it is those feelings which have stayed with me over the decades. Because, in my opinion, of all the seabird anglers, the terns are the most graceful, the most accomplished, and the most likely to lead a human angler to his or her quarry.

And there is another reason.

When the terns leave in the fall they fly across the equator; the arctic tern will keep flying until it reaches Antarctica. Most migratory birds follow the sun as the Earth tips on its axis and its declinations extend night in the northern hemisphere while days lengthen to the south. Terns are followers of the light. Aloft on those slim, dagger-shaped wings, tossed by trade winds and carried like white leaves blown along the sea's endless swells, they see more of the sun than any other creature. As icebound mammals of the Arctic prepare for endless days of darkness, the tern is already winging south toward the land of the midnight sun. And once there, it lingers for just a few weeks then departs as its blazing partner for life begins its return march north.

I have never been a friend of the night. As the terns leave, I wish I were with them, flying in the sun's blazing wake. And when, at last, the first terns bring the long suns of summer back to Middle Bay, they bring us the most joyous times of our year.

BLACK-CAPPED CHICKADEE
(*Parus atricapillus*)

Although I feel lonelier for the tern's equinoctial departure, the long, dark Maine winters that inevitably follow are brightened by another, quite different bird: the indomitable chickadee. "How long a Maine winter would be without our visits from the chickadee," I once wrote, and it's a line that has been quoted frequently.

Probably because it's true. As even casual observers have discovered, this is Maine's friendliest bird. Folks who buy their first experimental bag of sunflower seed and scatter it hopefully on their patio or back stoop are infallibly delighted when the first wild bird responds to the offering. Ninety-nine times out of a hundred, that bird is a chickadee.

It makes a splendid first impression. Trim, handsome, alert and animated, bold and sociable, the tiny creature is everything a birdwatcher hopes for. And for as long as seed and suet are dependably supplied, the chickadee will be back and will bring more than a few of its flock.

Through the bitter cold of winter's darkest days, the chickadee prevails. Quite unafraid of man or beast, it cocks its black-capped head and looks straight at every visitor, its tiny jet-black eyes aglow with bright evidence of an immortal, unquenchable inner spirit.

So strongly does that spirit radiate from such a small and apparently fragile creature that every man, woman or child who meets a chickadee in January is reassured that God must indeed be in his heaven and all will be right with the world. Given the guarantees that more snow will fall and more cold will march across the night, such confident reassurances are most gratefully received.

Such bravado in the face of winter's worst is reason enough to love the chickadee, yet the bird has more virtues to be discovered. Indeed, this is a creature that comes close to being totally virtuous, if you can imagine such a thing.

Like its global family, the black-capped chickadee has had ample time to perfect its good behavior. A resident of the northern pine forests since the Tertiary Period some 25 million years ago, chickadee ancestors followed those forests across the top northern half of the planet when the continents were still joined and before the Bering Sea divided North America from Asia. There are close cousins of today's chickadee in the dense conifers of Siberia, although most of them are not treated to generous handouts of sunflower seed.

Whenever and wherever it comes in contact with humans, the chickadee has made fast friends. The bird is part of the lore and legend of almost every American Indian tribe that ranged the northern latitudes. Surely the chickadee's defiance of winter's worst is part of the reason. When brutal snows and mortal cold send most creatures undercover, these conditions prompt the chickadee to seek the company of humankind. Whether it be a trapper's campfire, a remote farmhouse, or the back porch of a suburban split-level, any place where people are is a place chickadees will elect to spend their winters.

With good reason. Primarily insect eaters during the temperate seasons, chickadees must radically shift their diet to seeds and nuts after the first hard frosts force grubs, beetles, moths, worms, and their buggy brethren into hidden hibernation. To survive, chickadees gather as many seeds as they can and stash them in dozens of hollows and hiding places across their territories.

How can they remember every hidey hole? Recent researchers

have one answer. Triggered by the same first frosts that prompt insects to seek snug shelters, chickadees actually enlarge their memory circuits, adding new cells to their hippocampal neurons, the
part of their brains that energizes memory. This wondrously
evolved cerebral renewal gives this apparently vulnerable creature
an edge on winter by helping it remember the locations of its mul-
titude of seed stashes.

Of course, if the chickadees are resourceful enough to locate a
backyard feeder or two, those hippocampal neurons get a rest; even
an absentminded chickadee can remember the location of a free
lunch. And not merely from one day to the next, but from winter
to winter. With a life span of twelve years, the chickadee that greets
you one October is quite likely to have met you years before.

Seldom more than five inches long and weighing about as
much as a two-page letter, this is a bird that defies logic when it appears just outside your window as the thermometer sticks at zero
degrees Fahrenheit. You are inside in your longies staying close to
the stove; the chickadee is out there in the arctic wind dressed, apparently, in nothing more than the same feathers it wore last summer. What you cannot see is the extra layer of fat that the chickadee's metabolic controls have installed during the night. Nor can
you tell that beneath those exterior feathers there is a winter coat
of insulating down as fine as any that pads your ski parka. Nevertheless, in order to maintain these and other cold-defeating mech-
anisms, chickadees need plenty of fuel. If you'd care to count, you
can plan on a feeding budget of about 250 sunflower seeds per bird
per day during winter's meanest months.

Never fear: the chickadees will return the favor. Just watching
the effortless acrobatics that are part of this creature's daily reper-
toire will cheer even the chilliest soul. On the wing, a chickadee can
loop the loop; on a perch, this show-off will complete what's called
the giant swing—in this instance, somewhat of a misnomer for the
little chickadee's full-circle maneuver. Upside down, sideways, and
right-side up, every posture seems as easily maintained as any other
for the constantly moving chickadee, the limitless energies of its
performance given so generously that its audience must applaud.

It is at moments like these that we wonder how dark our winters might be without the splendid chickadees.

When winter finally eases into early spring, the chickadee flock begins its gradual return to the woods and fields. The tribe of twenty-five or thirty birds that gathered each morning at your backyard feeder divides into pairs as April and May glide so reassuringly onto the calendar. Seeking out, or returning to, hollowed compartments seldom more than twelve feet above ground in dead trees—old birches are preferred—chickadee parents prepare for their broods. Their hidden nests are elegantly lined with horsehair, fleece, grass, moss, and feathers; from five to nine white eggs speckled with brown are laid. Each about the size of a modest grape, they will hatch in time to allow the average chickadee parents to send their first brood out into the world and have a second batch of eggs in the nest by July.

These are busy days for the parents. In addition to feeding themselves, they are constant providers for their brood. And it is as they discharge their parental obligations that these minute dynamos grant us their most beneficial service. These foraging parents are champion insect finders and consumers, and the bugs they swallow are, for the most part, pests with penchants for ravaging vegetable and flower gardens, orchards, fruit, and much of the greenery that enhances Maine's brief summers.

A single pair of chickadee parents, observed by Massachusetts ornithologist Edward Howe Furbush, made six visits to their nest within thirteen minutes. Each time their bills were packed with small insects: plant lice, spiders, ants, and mayflies. This routine goes on all day long, and the number of insect casualties is up in the thousands. The tiny stomach of a single bird contained more than 450 plant lice. So not only are we blessed with the chickadee's winter cheer, but all during those summer months when the bird is out of our ken it is destroying gypsy-moth larvae, plant lice, ants, spiders, flea beetles, tent caterpillars, bark beetles, codling moths, cankerworm moths, leaf hoppers, and bark lice, to name a few.

And because it has the energy, the small bill, and the determination to dig out insect eggs buried beneath bark or shielded in other ways, the chickadee's insect-control program is one of the few that beats bugs before they hatch. Unlike many other of our feathered friends, the chickadee is not tempted by the ripening fruits that you have gone to such trouble to husband. Indeed, it would be difficult to name another wild creature who gives so much and asks so little.

When its summer responsibilities have been dutifully discharged and October's first convincing frosts announce the challenging season just offstage, chickadees reassemble their territorial flocks and begin their seed harvests. Doing so, they bring us yet another bonus, for this is also the time when many warblers begin stoking their metabolic engines for their fall migrations far to the south. Many of these exotic travelers keep close company with chickadee flocks, knowing that wherever the little gray bird goes, food will most likely turn up. Which is why, when autumn leaves begin to color, you will see flashes of brilliant yellow among the more modest plumage of the chickadees.

Soon afterward, when the last of the leaves have fallen and ice clogs the woods ponds, chickadees will return to your feeder, prepared yet again to cheer you through the winter. They will, if you can whistle their two-note call, respond in kind. Given a bit of patience, they will take seeds from your open hand, from your hat brim, and even from between your lips. For this is not only a brave, industrious, cheerful, pest-destroying, playful, handsome, acrobatic, defiant, energetic, trustworthy, charming and musical bird; it is one that seems to truly enjoy your company. If there is more that any of us can ask from a wild creature, I swear I don't know what it can be.

There is something you can give in return. Chickadees respond well to the presence of nesting boxes: small, simple wooden structures—a box with a slanted roof and a hole about an inch-and-a-half in diameter in the center of the front side. One panel should be hinged so the nesting box can be opened and cleaned during the off season. Line the bottom with cotton, and put the box out in the fall (not more than twelve feet off the ground) so the chickadees can check it out during the winter. The odds are excellent that you will host a fine chickadee family or two during the following spring and summer. If the birds appear reluctant to take advantage of your open house, station a bit of suet near the nesting-box entrance. The return on this modest investment, as the chickadee has so often demonstrated, will be more than most of us deserve.

GREAT HORNED OWL
(*Bubo virginianus*)

Winter's counterpoint to the chickadee is the great horned owl. While the chickadee is sociable, amusing, and friendly to humankind, the great horned owl is belligerent and predatory, and has, in fact, attacked men, women, children, and their pets. And while the humans suffered from fright and lacerations of the scalp and arms, most of the pets were killed. Of all the birds on my life list, this is the most awesome, one of the largest and most mystical, and the one that sets my heart to pounding whenever we meet.

Consider this true story from my home state.

"I heard this kind of soft *woosh* over my head. Next thing I knew, this big owl came down and nailed Bandit and went straight up in the air with him. I couldn't believe it. This thing had grabbed my dog."

Bob Shufelt, a fifty-four-year-old sawmill worker from Greenville, Maine, had taken Bandit out for his usual early morning walk. It was January's first week; the sun had yet to rise, and a reluctant dawn was gray and gloomy.

And there went Bandit, a twenty-pound dog with long white hair, offspring of a Pekinese and a poodle, carried thirty feet off the ground, clutched in the talons of a great horned owl: the tiger of the air.

"I yelled and ran after the owl, and it dropped Bandit. But it

was too late to save my dog. That owl turned and hissed at me, · spread its wings."

The belligerent bird terrorized Greenville well into the forenoon, attacking one of Shufelt's neighbor's cats and later swooping down on two senior citizens walking toward town.

This was not the first time the "Greenville owl" had been seen in the neighborhood. Since Christmas the bird had snacked on several cats and suburban squirrels. But after the attacks on the pet pekinoodle and two elderly pedestrians, folks decided it was time to call for help. Sergeant Pat Dorion, a regional game warden, arrived and shot the owl.

"I've taken some heat," he said later, "but the town was in an uproar. People came to my office and said they were going to get out there with their shotguns. We thought it best to do the job ourselves, rather than having folks running around town with guns."

The dead bird weighed 3½ pounds, yet it had carried off a twenty-pound pekinoodle. Pound for pound, ounce for ounce, the great horned owl is the nation's most aggressive bird of prey. Verified, eyewitness tales of the owl's ferocity are told across the country where *Bubo viginianus* has lived unchallenged by all creatures except humankind for some 36 million years.

During my decades as a Maine journalist, the great horned owl has been the topic of many excited, often outraged, telephone calls. A friend from Waldoboro phoned several times one winter to report the decimation of her flock of prize bantams. Another victim reported that each of his three cats had vanished, one after the other. He was certain it was *Bubo*'s terrible work.

My friend Stuart Vorpahl, a fisherman from Amagansett, Long Island, once kept two great horned owls as pets in his backyard aviary. After one of them sunk its talons into Stuart's hand, digging deep through the welder's glove he wore, he released the birds. Within a week, not one of Stuart's neighbor's fifteen cats and kittens could be found anywhere.

They are fearless and magnificent birds of prey, these large gray owls with their huge yellow eyes; dark, barred stripes; great round heads topped by a pair of feathered tufts that are their "horns"; and intricately feathered wings that spread five feet or more, allowing the bird to glide swiftly, silently through the pine groves it favors.

Ever voracious, the great horned patrols a feeding territory of up to six square miles and will dine on just about anything that moves, either diurnally or nocturnally. Rabbits, snakes, opossums, raccoons, squirrels, domestic fowl, cats and dogs, mice, voles, hares, ducks, and geese are all on *Bubo's* menu. As are skunks, the great horned being one of the planet's very few creatures who is not dissuaded by a skunk's odoriferous defense. Even porcupines are not immune; great horneds have been found with quills spiked in their breasts.

With its keen vision; razored talons; hooked beak; broad, silent wings; and fearless, aggressive attitude, Bubo has no airborne equal when it comes to killing. Even humans are vulnerable to attack; there are many records of lacerated scalps to prove it. This is, indeed, the tiger of the air.

Yet here in northern New England, there are reasons to love it. On January dusks as I walk the path through our woods to the frozen river in the chill twilight of the Wolf Moon, there is scarcely a sound beyond my footsteps, soft in the pine needles. Then a wild voice stops me. Gruff, pitched low, it could almost be the bark of a distant hound. "*Whoo, whoo-oo, whoo, whoo . . .*" It is close by, somewhere in the shadowed forest. Then another, a response, from another part of the woods, this time lower, more strung out. Awesome to hear on this icy evening, the thermometer far below freezing.

It is a pair of great horned owls and these are their courting calls, soon to blend into a husky exchange. Such are the voices of creatures who defy winter, who somehow remain undaunted by hissing sleet or snowstorms that roll like blustery seas across the open fields. This is weather that renders most creatures mute. Squirrels no longer chatter; lesser birds have flown south. Partridge flap their way into shelters beneath the evergreens, and bears are sodden in their dens.

Yet out here, back in these deep, piney woods, aloft in the tallest pine where a deserted squirrel's nest rests in that tree's high hollow, an owl mother-to-be is muttering words of love. This is what I hear, this guttural, primordial sound that drapes the winter evening with its feral presence. These are the voices of the pirates of the night, creatures fierce enough, proud enough, and so un-afraid that they say, "Here we are." It is their voices, and theirs alone, that tell me these woods are still wild and alive.

For January's deepest cold is the owl's spring. While the bear sleeps and fish lie still as stones in the river's darkest depths, the great horned kills and loves. In a week or so, the female will pluck a few feathers from her pale breast to soften the bed of the hollow where she nests. Before February is gone, three eggs will rest on those feathers, and while Yankees wonder if spring has forgotten them, the newborn cubs of the air will teeter on high boughs, get-ting their first look at the woods they are born to rule.

Years ago, on another winter dusk, I sat dark against a bench at the end of our point, which poked like a long finger into a frozen bay. In the deepening twilight a soundless shadow crossed the sky, wheeled, and came to rest on the branch of a single wind-scarred oak that had held its ground atop the bluff.

That branch was less than ten feet from my head, and I looked into the wide, yellow eyes of a great horned owl, come silent from the skies, silhouetted there against the last light in the west.

I was uneasy with our meeting, but that bird was implacable. As it stood there immobile on the branch, its eyes burned the night away, pinned to mine as if it brought me a message on those great, broad wings. That was as close as I have ever come to such a fierce, wild bird of prey, free in that lonely place to do whatever it willed. I sat very still.

Five minutes, ten, perhaps an eternity passed before that owl opened its wings against the gathering night, dipped off the limb, turned toward me for a heart-thumping moment, then swooped across the end of the point, a dark shadow gliding along the bay's pale, frozen rim until it vanished in the woods across the cove.

But of course, I see it still.

Northern Cardinal
(*Cardinalis cardinalis*)

Like the chickadee, the cardinal is a bird that nourishes our spirits during the short, often bleak days of Maine's unforgiving winters. For that, and its willingness to make almost daily house calls, it is a bird much beloved by New Englanders, who live at the edge of the cardinal's northernmost range.

Each year, it seems, the limits of that range are pushed a bit farther north. Like dozens of other warm-weather species whose infrequent northeastern appearances were once limited to states south of Long Island or Pennsylvania, the cardinal has joined the egret, the ibis, the turkey vulture, and others on their journeys to northern New England—a venue where they were complete strangers a half-century ago. When I first arrived in Maine around the middle of the twentieth century, the sight of a bright-red bird in the heart of a bitter cold January would have caused all sorts of excitement at the regional Audubon Society and other bird-watching organizations.

Less than fifty years later, the remarkable presence of this dramatically and unmistakably crimson creature, brilliant against the blinding white of new snow under a January sun, brings joy to all who share it. But the bird generates little or no interest among serious ornithologists. "Oh yes," they'll say when you describe an all-red bird, "almost surely a cardinal. We have quite a few wintering here now." As if there isn't that much to get excited about.

So much for science.

Scientists must honor fact, but the romanticists among us see the cardinal in winter as a symbol of vitality, a rose that blooms in defiance of every killing frost. Even if it is what meteorologists label global warming that brings the red bird to the north woods, its arrival is still considered something of a miracle by the old-timers who have endured scores of Yankee winters without a cardinal's comforting appearance at their window bird feeders. You have to live with those winters for a while before you can understand what a difference a bird can make.

I know. Jean and I have fed the birds for almost forty years; except for our Key West hiatus, we've never missed a winter. And most of that food has been purchased at Brooks Feed & Farm, a friendly store that stocks its shelves with everything an owner of animals, birds, fish or reptiles might need—everything. And there were times when we owned almost everything: horses, a burro, parakeets, canaries, dogs, cats, rabbits, chameleons, turtles, tropical fish, gerbils, and guinea pigs. At Brooks Feed & Farm, they know me well.

These days, I am there for birds alone. The children who were the principle owners of each of the species in our menagerie now have sons, pets, and mortgages of their own. Still, I think of them as I wander the aisles at Brooks and stop for a look at colorful tanks filled with even more colorful exotica from tropical seas. There are always children at Brooks. There is obviously a relationship between children and pets, a quirk of human nature when you stop to think about it: Why would parents who have their time consumed by two or three school-age sons and daughters want to add parakeets and poodles to their already hectic households? As one who has been through it, I'm still not able to comprehend the reasoning. Still, the children's enthusiastic chatter cheers me as I shop for seed and suet.

And there's plenty of company in my age bracket, too. On a recent visit, as I was loading the scale with two pounds of thistle seed, a definitely senior fellow approached me. "Will cardinals eat that?" he asked.

"Well, they might," I replied. "But I've never seen them try it. They always go for the sunflower seed."

"You mean like that?" he asked, pointing to a drum full of black sunflower seeds.

"That's the stuff. They love it."

As I left, he was carefully weighing up precisely one pound. I supposed he didn't want to invest too much on his first try, and on the advice of a stranger, at that.

Each morning when I see the cardinal making his cautious approach to our feeder—he never flies right in like the chickadees—I think of that fellow. "They're such pretty birds," he told me. "A red bird like that could sure cheer up my winter. I hope I can get one to stop by." I've been crossing my fingers that a cardinal will, in fact, pay him a visit, and I've been looking for this would-be bird-watcher at Brooks. For what he said caught the essence of getting to know birds better: it's good for one's soul. And a brilliant crimson presence that defies snow and sleet is among the best there is.

Jean and I have been blessed. Ever since we moved here near the banks of the Androscoggin River, a pair of cardinals has made regular visits to our feeding station. They are, we have discovered, also nesting nearby. In late September, the young-of-the-year show up to try out sunflower seeds on their own. The adolescent male has yet to grow into his father's brilliant crimson; just hints of what's to come are there, mixed with the nondescript plumage of childhood. The young miss is also dressed modestly, but already she is trim, neatly packaged, and almost as impressive as her mother. In many ways, the mature female cardinal is the most handsome of the two, clad as she is in an impeccably sleek, buff-colored suit touched with creamy beige and accented by her striking red bill. Her beauty is both subtle and perfectly tailored, a step away from the brash and total redness of the male, which is, after all, a kind of overstatement, as if nature had forgotten its rules of protective coloration. Now that I think of it, that may be what makes the male so cautious; without hope of camouflage, he must be forever wary.

I am always grateful and relieved when the cardinal family begins its autumnal feeding schedule at the feeder. When the red bird vanishes during the summer, my anxieties simmer: it would be so easy, I tell myself, for a bird that visible to be picked off by a hawk, house cat, owl, or other equally efficient predator. But so far we and the cardinals have been lucky. They return on schedule and, I've learned, with an excellent excuse for their absence.

In this family, both mother and father are equally diligent parents when it comes to caring for their infant hatchlings. The father, especially, is an untiring provider, and when at last the fledglings take wing for the first time, he is at their side. He flails his wings as he hops around, flitting from limb to limb, following every erratic move of his precious children. There may be other, more solicitous fathers in the avian world, but none live within the realm of our woods and fields, and surely none so proudly escorts its brood to our back porch.

Which would be reason enough to love the cardinal. But then, there is their song. The male sings well and often, a striking sound, as if a flawless crystal had been struck, a clear whistle, strong, unafraid, loud enough to fill the forest. Every now and then, the signature call slides into a sibilant hint of melody, but all is delivered with such vitality and pride that even though the bird is out of my sight, I can see its red breast puffed and its head high. His lady, on the other hand, has a more decorous voice, softer in tone, given more often to gentle improvisation. Together, theirs is some of the most memorable music in nature's collection.

It is just one more reason for my eternal gratitude that the cardinal family is part of our world. And why I hope for their return.

WILD TURKEY
(*Meleagris gallopavo*)

Glancing up from my breakfast cereal early one autumn morning, I was amazed, startled, and delighted to get my first look at a flock of wild turkeys in our own backyard. I could hardly believe my eyes. In my ornithological lexicon, these awesome birds are listed under exotica: creatures of Audubon's artistry, hallmarks of a Pilgrim Thanksgiving, or the target of Sergeant York's marksmanship in the long-ago wooded foothills of Tennessee. The brushy terrain that borders our yard here in Maine is most assuredly a long way from Tennessee. Yet here were these eighteen wild turkeys!

With binoculars in hand, I followed the flock's progress from east to west along the bank of the stream that borders our homestead. Fascinating. Lifting their long legs with a ballet dancer's grace, the big (I'll say!) birds took deliberate steps, pausing with each one to scratch, twice with the right foot, then once with the left. This was followed by a scan of the ground thus disturbed, and perhaps a quick peck or two. Everything was done energetically, purposefully, and steadily as the entire flock followed, one after the other, in a rhythmic feeding march. Every so often, one of their naked, pointed heads would rise and turn quickly back and forth, checking the terrain for any signs of danger.

Before I knew it (because these birds are so large they can cover a lot of ground with relatively few of those long steps), they had vanished in the stand of white pine between our place and the river. I've seen the same flock several times since. I'm certain it's the same because it includes a partially albino hen. Her startling patch of snow-white feathers is quite unmistakable. But none of our meetings has been as dramatic as that first one.

Down the road, a friend who maintains well stocked bird feeders tells me two hen turkeys have visited him frequently during the winter. "The snow was so deep they couldn't walk through it," he told me, "so they flew in like bombers heading for a carrier. When they landed, they just flopped into the snow, leaving a dent that looked as if a barrel had fallen. I tossed out extra corn and they visited off and on until the end of March. Then one day they just stopped coming."

Which fits with the descriptions of wild-turkey behavior I get from ornithologists and biologists who study these big birds. Turkeys come to feeders during the deep winter, but when the snow starts thinning, they'll go back to their natural foods. And by March, wild turkeys have other matters on their minds. April and May are the bird's breeding season, a time when their behavior follows ancient and formal patterns.

Hens become affectionate and signal tom turkeys in their vicinity with soft clucks. As you might expect, the toms are listening hard for just such a signal, and their hearing is superb.

With his chest puffed up—and bolstered by a layer of fat called a "breast sponge," acquired for extra energy during the breeding season—the gobbler approaches, hoping he's charming enough to add yet another hen to his spring harem.

He gobbles: a unique, stirring series of liquid high notes, unforgettable and unmistakable. When he knows the hen is watching, he begins his dance—an extravagant courtship display. His wattles and caruncles, the entire featherless head and neck, change color from white to turquoise to blue to pink, purple, orange, and flaming red. He struts and puffs (Audubon called it a *pfum*) and spreads his tail feathers like a peacock. With his head arched so far back it rests against those tail feathers, he walks with slow and measured steps toward the hen, drags his wings along the ground, and gobbles on until, if he has been properly impressive, the hen signals she won't kick him out. But it will still be a while before she lets the proceedings evolve to more serious goings-on.

Once the dance passes its moment of ultimate passion, and this is indeed just a moment, the tom begins his quest for yet another hen. A few weeks later, the hen constructs a shallow, almost primitive nest on the ground and begins to lay her pale buff eggs, often splotched with brown. She adds one each day until there are from twelve to fourteen. As the brood begins to hatch twenty-eight days later, the sire tom and any of his cronies are definitely *persona non grata*. He and his fellow gobblers gather some distance off in the woods, where they become dispirited, slovenly bachelors, just hanging out, doing very little that's useful.

But as autumn takes hold and the first frosts chill the forest floor, the flock reassembles and command is turned over to the oldest, strongest gobbler, which can weigh twenty-five pounds or more. By then, those young-of-the-year turkeys have become adolescents, able to shift for themselves. The hens weigh from eight to ten pounds and the teen toms, called jakes, from twelve to fourteen. It is during these cooler months that wild turkeys are most active, eating as much and as often as they can, stocking up for winter. After a sizeable flock has visited the forest floor under a stand of acorn-bearing oaks, the ground looks as if it's been tilled.

When the snows do come, these impressive birds are patient and resourceful. Often they'll stay perched on their tree-limb roosts for as long as five or six days, whatever it takes for the storms to ease and the snowdrifts to settle. In many parts of their northern range, wild turkeys have become fast friends of the white-tailed deer, sticking close to the herds and roosting near deer yards, where snows are trampled down and food is easier to find.

These are not the foolish birds that domestic, farm-raised turkeys have become. These are true wild creatures whose genes have equipped them to deal with harsh winters and the several predators that pursue them. Of these, the great horned owl is the enemy wild turkeys most fear.

For this owl is a certain killer. Flying silent through the deep night into a turkey roost, the owl will perch alongside a sleeping bird. Then it hoots. Startled, the turkey moves a few paces out, toward the end of the roosting limb. The owl follows, then hoots again. The deadly duet ends when the turkey reaches the end of the branch and must take flight. As it spreads its wings, the owl pounces.

But natural predators and strictly regulated hunting seasons in some states have not hindered the wild turkey's amazing comeback, a restoration that represents one of the most successful in wildlife-management history. Abundant enough in colonial New England to become the Pilgrim's feasting dish, the great bird had all but vanished by the late 1880s in the wake of unrestricted hunting and the clear-cutting of much of the nation's hardwood forest for farmland.

Ironically, it is the few remaining farms, especially the diary operations, that have aided the resilient wild turkey's return. Helped by state wildlife biologists in much of the northeast, the birds that have been introduced to farm habitats soon find plenty of the corn that's cultivated as cattle feed. In Maine, for example, where a few wild birds were transplanted from Vermont less than twenty-five years ago, there is now a wild-turkey population of more than four thousand birds, including the eighteen I was so delighted to see from our kitchen window. At current growth rates, the Maine wild-turkey census will soon count as many birds as there were in the "good old days."

If you have yet to meet your first wild turkey, believe me, you will be impressed. There simply isn't another American bird around that's as large or dressed in such impressive bronze and black feathers. With its curving neck and small head above an oval torso that tapers to a slim tail, this is a noble, most impressive wild creature. I have counted myself lucky ever since that breakfast glance at our backyard.

BALTIMORE ORIOLE
(Icterus galbula)

T hat first summer after our good neighbor Arthur Hummer retired from his twenty-five years at the shipyard, he spent much of his time fishing for striped bass from the shores of Middle Bay. And although I was not retired—and probably never will be—I also spent many of those summer hours on the banks of the bay, fishing rod in hand and expectations high. There are many less satisfactory ways to pass the time.

For reasons I have never fully understood, Arthur brought more stripers ashore than I, even though, in my opinion, his fishing gear and technique were primitive. In the process of trying to discover his secrets, I also discovered more about Arthur. I visited him at his home more often and we talked of many things. And after every visit I told myself how little I had really known of this gentle, shy, and straightforward man of Maine.

I asked about his years in the shipyard: what the work was like, building great steel ships of war. Arthur said he had never intended to spend so much of his life there; he went to work in World War II because the yard needed all the help it could get to build the destroyers that would become the Allies' first line of defense against Axis U-boats.

"But when the war ended, I just stayed on," Arthur told me. "The pay was good. And after a while I got used to being inside those steel hulls.

"The work didn't help my hearing none," he said, looking at me with his small, shy smile. "I miss the bird songs. All that music of the spring. Can't hear none of it no more."

I thought about that as I walked home from my visit. It was a short walk, about a quarter-mile. But there were no other houses along the way, just tall pines sighing in the breeze, and bird songs. I wondered what it would be like not to be able to hear the sounds of nature.

Twenty years later, I found out. My ears had suffered from a childhood bout with scarlet fever and from scores of high-altitude missions in Army Air Force planes during the same war that Arthur spent building destroyers. But my hearing began to slip away so gradually I never noticed the loss. I found myself saying "What?" more often than ever, yet it was not until I realized I no longer heard bird songs that I told myself I was going deaf. I had discovered the same silence Arthur had known for years. And the same sadness.

It was the Baltimore oriole's music I missed most, for several reasons. Because Maine is at the northernmost edge of the oriole's range, the brilliant orange-and-black male and the more subtle—but in some ways more lovely—olive-brown and burnt-orange female do not arrive until late in the first week of May, or early in the second. I've been keeping notes on the first oriole's arrival for more than twenty years, and May 11 is the most popular date, with more than a half-dozen entries.

We have learned, as a great many other oriole fans have also discovered, that a half an orange spiked to a tree trunk is a proven oriole attractor. So on the fifth of May, or thereabouts, I put up the first orange halves; then we wait and watch. One morning, out of nowhere, that stunning flash of orange and black appears as the oriole flies unerringly to the orange, perches there, and darts its slim, sharp bill into the fruit. Section by section, the bird neatly consumes every edible bit. During that first week, I must replace the empty halves with fresh ones each day. After ten days or so, the bird's orange addiction tapers off and soon stops altogether. Why the appetite is so avid at first is one more natural mystery that may happily go unsolved.

The moment of the oriole's arrival is especially sweet because it tells us so convincingly that Maine's long, damp, gray, chill, and disappointing spring is over and that early summer, with its soft, bright days and the fresh green of leafy trees has, at last, come to pass. Every year Jean is so impatient, so desperate for the change that she hears orioles singing when none are there.

"There's an oriole," she tells me in mid-April, cupping her ear with one hand and pointing toward the high trees with the other. "You better put out some oranges."

"It's early, too early," I say. But because I cannot hear the song she has heard, I cannot argue with conviction. Up go the oranges, much to the red squirrels' delight. The process has become as much a spring ritual as listening for the first peepers or watching for the osprey's return to our skies.

Weeks later, the orioles themselves prove beyond any doubt that they are back. We have more than one pair now. They like it here and build their nests, those intricately woven, deep-bottomed, swinging pouches, nearby to let us know they are content to raise their families in our neighborhood. Where the female finds the considerable amount of material she needs to weave her master-piece is beyond me. We have several old nests that we leave for the birds to recycle, nests that were dislodged and blown down by winter storms. But oriole mothers are choosy.

I watched the other day as one female tugged and tugged at a nylon leader on one of my fly rods in its rack on our back porch. She never was able to take any part of it but kept trying for the longest time, even though we had hung an old nest just a few feet away. As I have learned from examining those nests, oriole mothers have a preference for synthetics; perhaps it's because there are so many manmade fibers in our culture. At any rate, soon the nests may be quite non-biodegradable, and if storms don't wrench them from their high branches, they will become homes for many oriole generations.

I have, just this year, been fitted with a new hearing aid, one that's tuned to the fairly high frequencies of an oriole's song. These are the champion composers of the avian world, able to improvise melodies that become their own. The woods are no longer silent for me; I can share the oriole's rich and liquid music once again.

RUBY-THROATED
HUMMINGBIRD
(Archilochus colubris)

Most of the folks I see buying bird feeders and feeding supplies are older. That's a fact I never thought much about until I grew older myself. Sure, there are young people interested in birds, but theirs is a serious avocation. They will become ornithologists or biologists—scientists of some sort— or perhaps nature writers like my friend Peter Matthiessen, whose birding enthusiasm when we were in college helped so much to open my eyes to the natural presences around me.

I'm grateful for that. I've had a kind of head start. Even so, I was well into my sixties before I made a serious commitment to arranging and stocking a year-round bird feeding station. For one thing, we seniors put in more time at breakfast. My neighbor Brad, still in his forties and quivering with ambition, skips breakfast altogether. On his early-morning rush to get where he's going he barely has time to whip past the drive-in window at Dunkin' Donuts. There's no way he's going to spend even a minute of his morning watching birds.

But he'll come around, unless stress gets the best of him early on. There was a time when I rushed from cold cereal and coffee to my desk at the newspaper, properly convinced that my job was the most important part of my life and the several lives of our household. Oh, I took note of birds, but from the car window much more often than the kitchen window.

Self-employed now, I "go to work" in an office just a few steps from the kitchen. Proximity, in this case, does little for efficiency. Indeed, I tend to abuse the fact that the office awaits and will continue to do so without so much as a whisper, no matter how tardy my arrival. I linger at breakfast, and consider the meal incomplete without several cups of coffee and the full consumption of the morning's newspapers.

And, of course, the birds. We have never had better bird-watching than the spectacle we've enjoyed from our kitchen window ever since we moved to our current home several years ago. It's the combination of natural habitat that does it: tall stands of white pine, marshes, a stream, mature hardwoods, acres of farm-land and overgrown pasture just across our road, and the broad reaches of the lower Androscoggin River a few steps beyond our backyard. Each provides a variety of wild environments for at least a hundred different species. Some are here year-round; most arrive and depart on fairly rigid seasonal schedules.

It was the hummingbird's schedule that moved me to buy a "nectar" dispenser at Brooks Feed & Farm. According to my calendar of migratory arrivals, the first hummingbirds show up at our place at the start of the second week in May. For years, those sightings had been chance glimpses of this smallest of birds hovering for a split second at one of Jean's blooming geraniums in its pot on the back porch. It always seemed too fleeting a moment; I wanted more of this fascinating creature. When I saw the feeder designed solely for hummingbirds, I bought it. Just like that.

This purchase, I have come to realize, was one more brick of evidence mortared into place as part of the foundation of my thesis that the length of time spent with birds increases in direct relationship to the watcher's age: the older, the longer, you could say. And waiting for and watching a ruby-throated hummingbird feeding from a nectar dispenser is a delightfully time-consuming process.

There the birds are, just inches from the sliding glass door that opens onto the back porch. If I stand at the door looking out, I am less than a foot from a ruby-throat, able to see its minute, dark dot of an eye and the iridescent red collar that adorns the male. Hovering, backing, darting, and dipping, this bird defines ultimate flight. There are no challengers to the hummingbird's mastery of the air; no other bird can fly as fast, none can hover or flip into and out of reverse and forward speeds with such artless dexterity. Watch them for any length of time and you find yourself forgetting they are birds. You tend to think of them as a separate life form, unique unto themselves.

But birds they are. They breed, nest, lay eggs, raise their young, and migrate in an ornithological duplication of the patterns followed by the oriole or the osprey. It's just that hummingbirds are so exquisitely tiny and so irrefutably exotic.

Their nests are the size of a small teacup, woven from spiderwebs and bits of lichen, lined with the finest down. Early in June, Mrs. Ruby-throat lays two eggs, no more, no less, the size of a pair of small peas. When they hatch in fourteen days or so, the hummingbird newborns could fit in a teaspoon, with room to spare. But with food pumped into them from their mother's long, slender bill, these tiniest siblings are ready to fly in less than a month.

While the mother—as is the case with almost all birds—does most of the family chores, the father hummingbird guards their nest with remarkable pugnacity, especially for such a mite. But in this case, smallness matters not. An aggressive, contentious sort and a bully—if that word can be used for a creature that weighs little more than a dime—male ruby-throats will chase all intruders, from bumblebees to crows. They are especially hard on other hummingbirds who wander into their territories. That needle of a beak, combined with blinding speed and awesome maneuverability, is more than enough to discourage every invader, even humans if they come too close to the nest.

Taken all around, however, the hummingbird is a friend of man. That slim, probing bill does more than siphon nectar. Whenever a ruby-throat appears to be sipping from a flower's interior, it is also consuming scores of very small insects, primarily newborn spiders.

But this bird of many virtues is also, like most of us, fallible. Once, as Jean and I both watched, a visiting male ruby-throat appeared to be flying erratically. Often, as it attempted to sip from blossoms on our honeysuckle vine, it missed the flower altogether, jerked into reverse, took aim and tried again, and missed again. I thought perhaps it suffered from some ailment affecting its co-ordination. After all, a hummingbird's brain is smaller than the head of a match; by my logic, it shouldn't take more than a bad cold to upset such a delicate mechanism.

As it turns out, that hummingbird was drunk, intoxicated, not ill. I learned from a true ornithologist that late in its blooming, especially if the sun is strong and warm, the sugar in honeysuckle nectar can ferment—can, in fact, become an alcoholic beverage. And like all such potables, too much consumed in too short a time can affect coordination, vision, and behavior. The hummingbird we watched was staggering, just as we all do when we seriously overindulge at the bar.

Ever since that moment, I've loved these littlest birds even more.

Tree Swallow
(*Tachycineta bicolor*)

While the hummingbird has no peer in its ability to dart, hover, and reverse, the several members of the swallow family run a close second when it comes to airborne maneuverability. Of these small, trim, and so sleekly streamlined birds, the tree swallow is our most frequent visitor, and one of the most anxiously awaited.

Because it feeds exclusively on flying insects, the tree swallow does not arrive in northern states like Maine until it is assured of nourishment. Which means temperatures must be moderate enough to encourage a hatch of some sort: that propitious moment when egg cases deposited so painstakingly months before are opened by a sun that can transform primitive larvae into creatures as ethereal as the mayfly or as pestiferous as the black fly and mosquito.

So even though the tree swallow's arrival is a certain signal that we will soon be considered a blood supply the minute we step outdoors, the bird is also irrefutable, and welcome, proof that winter is over. Welcome enough to give the tree swallow's arrival a degree of importance far beyond its circumstance. After all, swallows have shown up every May since there were calendars, and for millennia before.

Which still does not diminish the joy we feel at our first sight of these graceful fliers stitching their swooping patterns across the sky, embroidering our first days of May with the reassurance of their return. In the years I've kept written records, May 3 is the most-favored day for Maine's arriving tree swallows. An ornithologist friend has told me these first birds are exclusively males and will not stay long. They are, evidently, on their way even farther north.

That I can believe, for these are restless birds. When the ladies arrive, the tree-swallow population stabilizes and I can count on seeing several each day, sometimes from the bathroom window I peer from in the morning as I'm shaving. More often, though, I spot them during the lingering evenings, when our swallows swoop endlessly over the lawn and the field across the road, filling their gaping mouths with mosquitoes and other small winged insects that rise from the warmed earth like dust from a beaten rug.

It is a sublime service these birds perform. Once I knew how many mosquitoes a single swallow can consume each day; the precise number eludes me now, but it is astonishing, up there in the hundreds. So in addition to marveling at this bird's remarkable mastery of the air, I am also always pleased by the knowledge that the swallow's eloquent flight nips so many bloodsuckers in the bud, as it were. All birds, in my opinion, enrich our environment and our lives, but few do so as directly and effectively as swallows.

But there is another aspect of their behavior that saddens me; indeed, it saddens me so much that I tend to forget the rush of elation I feel on sighting the first tree swallow of spring. It seems that the moment they whirl across our perception like spring spirits on the wind, the birds begin to make plans for their departure. They are rather like Groucho Marx, who made "Hello, I must be going," one of his signature lines.

The minute the young-of-the-year are feathered just enough to take their first tentative flights from their nesting box or a small tree hollow, the parents begin preparing for the return journey south. Their marvelous aerobatics continue, but not for as long as they did in May. By early July, if you live north of the Mason-Dixon line, you can see tree swallows beginning to gather on utility lines. One day there may be six or seven, then a few days later there'll be a dozen or more. By the end of July, the flocking swallows will number forty or fifty on a wire.

Most folks, I suppose, take pleasure in the sight. But many of them, I'll bet, don't see it as a sign of the approaching autumn. After all, the swallows are still with us. Just because they are lined up in long, perfect rows on a long-distance cable is no reason for lament. But lament I do, because in this land of such brief, sweet summers, those rows of swallows tell me this splendid season's end is inevitable.

Other more practical, less frivolous individuals wouldn't think twice about such an acknowledgment. Of course autumn follows summer and has done so ever since this earth began turning on its axis. To hope otherwise, to dream of an endless summer, is the occupation of fools, romantics, procrastinators, dreamers, and wishful thinkers like the grasshopper who sings away his summer while the ants gather food for their winter.

I have always been something of a grasshopper. It's a weakness, I know, a flaw I am reminded of each time I mourn the swallows who flock for their departure in July. July! A month, in my opinion, that represents the very essence of summer, a time when no thoughts of lengthening nights and shorter days should be accorded any recognition whatsoever.

But there those swallows are, perched above me in a line that each day underscores the inevitability of the autumnal equinox. If only they wouldn't start so early. After all, didn't they just get here?

Of course, if I lived near the savannas of the deep South, I could watch great flocks of thousands of tree swallows as they arrive in the fall for their annual escape from the cold and settle in like dark, whirling clouds.

COMMON EIDER
(*Somateria mollissima*)

T he coast of Maine is the only place in the nation where eiders nest and raise their young, an ornithological fact for which I have always been grateful. For it was the comic antics of the eider fledglings I've met on so many of my sails alone on Casco Bay that added so much enjoyment to those cruises.

Some twenty-five years ago, when I read that a Portland yacht broker had become Hobie Alter's exclusive sales agent in Maine, I called him within the hour. I'd never seen a Hobie Cat, but I had read about it and had looked longingly at splendid, four-color photographs of the ingeniously designed catamaran soaring over great Pacific swells off the California beaches where the boat had been born. Within days, I became the first fellow in Maine to sail his very own Hobie 14 on Casco Bay.

With her two slim fiberglass hulls—gracefully molded to duplicate the streamlined shape of the outriggers on those Pacific war canoes we saw in so many B movies—the Hobie 14 was indeed a radical boat for her time. And Casco Bay was the perfect place to sail her. With its lacework shoreline of points and long peninsulas, there isn't enough fetch to allow swells of any size. When the wind blows, it puffs up whitecaps but no curling seas.

Which is the best of all Hobie worlds. With plenty of wind but no seriously rough water, that small sailboat literally flew. Her windward hull would rise, she would heel almost to her capsize point, and we would be hissing along at close to twenty knots. Several times I passed lobster boats under full power, much to the amazement of their skippers, who often did a double-take as I hustled by.

The Hobie was just as much fun on days when the wind was gentle, arriving easily from the southwest, cool off the Atlantic. After long tacks south to the open sea, I could turn for home with the breeze on my stern, sailing easily downwind with very little to do as I sat lazily on the canvas deck, the Hobie's long tiller in one hand.

This was the course for meeting eiders. Because the Hobie slipped so gently along, she made scarcely a sound. And because the eider broods sometimes numbered close to two dozen as one hen took on the offspring of several of her nesting associates, I could spot the juvenile flocks from a ways off. If I lay still on the canvas deck, those adolescent eiders seemed to have no fear of the Hobie—well, not until we were almost on top of them.

Then, when they realized too late that this apparition bearing down on them, this creature with the single, huge white wing, was on a collision course, the tiny sea ducks would dive. Which is what grown-up eiders do best, better than any other waterfowl. Several observers have clocked them at depths of sixty feet, and deeper. But those youngsters had neither the experience nor the density to make diving easy. About the size of a downy tennis ball, the juveniles would flip their tails up and paddle fiercely with tiny, webbed feet, flailing for purchase on the surface.

When, and if, they could actually begin to swim underwater, down they would go. By then, the Hobie and I were on top of them, surrounded by wiggling puffballs, or looking down into the crystal-clear water at the comic sight of a tiny sea duck swimming submerged for all it was worth, neck extended, feet thrashing like pistons. I would be past them before they surfaced, bobbing up in our gentle wake like corks, twisting their heads around for another look at the great, silent phantom that had taught them one of their first lessons in evasive tactics.

The fledglings' decision to wait until the last moment before taking cover reflects the generally trusting nature of eider adults. The large grown-ups, weighing close to five pounds with a wing-span of more than three feet, have never been classified as wary creatures. That and the succulence of their eggs, the dramatic white and black plumage of the males, and the famous eiderdown pur-loined from their nests were responsible for the near extinction of Maine's nesting population.

By the summer of 1907, according to Maine ornithologist Alfred O. Gross, the state's eider flock numbered just twenty birds, or fewer. That remnant of a once thriving population lived on a single offshore island far down east. But, in the wake of protective legislation, a ban on egg taking and on hunting, these icons of the state's open-ocean coast began one of the most remarkable come-backs in natural history. Gradual at first, eider restoration began to gain critical mass in the mid-1930s. By 1943, the ducks were nest-ing on thirty-one islands instead of a single, isolated dot off the coast. When I began sailing my Hobie Cat early in the sixties, there were some twenty thousand pairs nesting on a hundred and fifty islands, several of them in Casco Bay, where I often cruised on those splendid solo adventures.

Since then, the Hobie has been given to two sons, one after the other, and the youngest (whose job required him to leave Maine) passed it to a friend who lives on the bay in Portland. His dock is visible from the highway leading into the city, and if I'm driving by during the summer, I look across the water and often spot the Hobie, pulled up on the bank, still rakish after more than three decades. Every time I see her, I think of our adventures and our meetings with those eider infants.

Which, by the way, are now more numerous than ever. Accord-ing to biologist Brad Allen, who keeps track of Maine's native ei-ders for the Department of Inland Fisheries and Wildlife, there are more than thirty thousand breeding pairs, and their nesting grounds now occupy most of the suitable island habitats from the farthest eastern shores, southwest along the coast, to the very edge of Maine's border with New Hampshire. From the brink of extinc-tion, these rugged cold-water birds are now pushing their habitat envelope. There may be, in Brad Allen's words, about as many eiders as Maine can support.

On a recent visit to an offshore island, I stood by the wheelhouse of the lobsterboat that took me there and counted at least a thousand eiders. I made the trip in the early spring, and the birds were in their most handsome plumage. The males' black and white heads and elaborately hued bills were vivid, and their plaintive calls, a kind of slurred moaning, made a pervasive, wonderfully strange music I could hear from every quarter the moment the boat's engine was shut down as we reached the dock.

Everywhere I walked along that island's shore, I could see eiders on the water and hear their unique calls. It was like meeting old friends again. I wanted to ask if any of them remembered me from thirty years before, when they were just barely out of their nests and I sailed so silently above them in that splendid Hobie Cat: the first Hobie those eider kids had ever seen.

RED-WINGED BLACKBIRD

(*Agelaius phoeniceus*)

O ther than city skyscrapers, there are few places where you can awaken, walk to your bedroom window, and look *down* on birds as they fly by. But I shall never forget two of them, both on Maine-coast islands.

The first was Harry and Betsey's house on Gilbert Head, surely one of the most romantic sites on the entire Atlantic coast. Perched there like a great, gray gull, high on a bluff at the island's southeastern tip, that remarkable house looks out over the tumult of the Kennebec River's perpetual meeting with the open Atlantic. The great river's waters, which begin close to the Canadian border, become tidal at the Augusta dam some thirty miles from the sea, a geographic circumstance—this mixing of fresh and salt—which gives the lower Kennebec an exceptional fecundity.

Fish of many kinds, as well as their constant predators, are especially concentrated at the river's mouth, that place where tides and currents clash and the great house maintains its vigil above the unending tumult. Gulls are on patrol from dawn to dusk, gliding above the carnage, swooping to the surface, bickering over bits of flotsam and flesh that rise from the submerged struggles for survival.

So if you are high above the Kennebec, as I was in that corner bedroom, you can stand at a window to watch the sun rise, or the tides surge, and see gulls flying below you, or at eye level.

Fisherman Island off the coast at Boothbay Harbor, one river down east of the Kennebec, is also the site of a remarkable house. While Harry and Betsey's place is built of wood and looks as if it had grown from the headland soil, the house on Fisherman is all of stone: large rocks hauled from the burly stone walls that course here and there like veins and arteries bulging from the island's skin of fields and brush. Years before the Revolutionary War, the stones were piled there to pen ewes from rams, cows from bulls, and she-goats from billy goats. That was a time when offshore islands were thought to be safer than the mainland because they were places the Indians seldom visited.

More than two hundred years later, the Unitarian minister who owned Fisherman built the stone house from what was left of those walls. He never lacked for material, even though the place is large, almost like a castle. Two high-ceilinged, soaring stories tall, it stands impressively on the island's highest hilltop with windows on all sides. No matter where you are inside, you can look out and see the ocean that surrounds you.

I know, because the island's new owner—a charming and successful fellow—invited us to spend a few days at the stone mansion as his guests. Which is how it happened that one morning as I was shaving, I peered out the bathroom window and found myself looking down at a red-winged blackbird flying below.

For me, that was a stunning and poignant sight, one that soared far, far back into the deepest reaches of my memories.

For there was much about the interior of that house at Fisherman that spoke to me of another place—the house on Georgica Pond where I spent summers as an infant, a child, a boy, and a young man. Just as that was a summer house, its airy rooms with their white walls and pale curtains billowing in the southwest breeze, so too is the Fisherman mansion a place for the summer, with the same pale walls, white wicker furniture, and soft, damp smell of the sea.

That house on Georgica has never ceased its singing deep in

the innermost springs of my memory. Never. How often I return in my dreams, whether day or night. And it is the red-wing, along with a half-dozen other birds, that plays a key role in the endless drama of my most distant past as it unfolds over and over again on the softly lit stage I see when I look within.

It was my grandfather who loved that place most, and it was his love I learned to share. He yearned for the house on the pond as much as I did during my grade-school days.

In March, when he could wait no longer to open the place at Georgica, my grandfather—with Granny at his side—would stop by school on a Friday afternoon and ask the headmaster to set me free for the weekend. I'd rush down the stairs toward the elegant, waiting Packard, and off we'd go.

Without central heat in those days, the house in March had to be warmed with a combination of fireplaces and stoves that burned either kerosene or coal. The largest kerosene stove was in the dining room. As big as a steamer trunk, it sat there on the hearth, gurgling every now and then as fuel flowed into its flaming interior. My grandfather called it Florence, the name, I think, of the manufacturer. On those evenings of our very first arrival, we would share a supper of cold roast-beef sandwiches and milk, with our chairs pulled close to each other at the end of the table nearest the stove. When I looked out the window, I could see Georgica gleaming silver gray in the dusk.

But on those bright, brisk March mornings, after we had breakfast in the kitchen by the coal stove, the pond would be a brilliant blue, flecked with whitecaps stirred by a gathering southwest wind. The high cattails bordering the shore waved in that wind, and as I walked toward them across the lawn I could hear the spring song of the male red-wing: "*kong . . . ger . . . eee*" with the emphasis on the last, rich, high note. He would be swaying there, clinging to the top of the tallest cattail stalk, apparently unfazed by the way it wobbled in the wind.

But as I came closer, the red-wing's call changed from a song to a kind of guttural "*chut, chut,*" a signal, I assumed, that sounded an alarm. And then, as I stood close, at the very edge of the reeds, he would spread his wings and fly in circles, never getting far from the territory he had staked as his own, and very probably the same spot he had claimed the same way for several years. And somewhere in that thick mass of cattails, his mate was building—or rebuilding—the nest where she would soon raise her brood.

As the male circled, the brilliant crimson of his feathered shoulders—his blazing epaulets—flashed in the sunlight, reminding me each time of the Indian legend of how this blackbird tucked glowing coals beneath its wings to save fire for an Indian nation all but destroyed by floods.

So vivid was that image, so poignant those schoolboy visits to Georgica in early spring, so filled with happiness were those days in the house that smelled of salt and stoves, that every March since I have watched for the red-wing's return from its wintering grounds to the south. Even when we could not live near water and the marshes the birds so favor, I would drive miles to a likely red-wing habitat just to listen for that exuberant spring song. For me, the red-wing has become a messenger from the long-ago, a symbol of the first pure happiness in my young life. And verifying its return each March certifies that boyhood joy.

But until my visit to Fisherman, I had never seen a red-wing from above, the flames on its wings more brilliant than ever. It is one more image safe now in my storehouse within.

White Ibis
(Eudocimus albus)

I f you have doubts about destiny, then you might want to review the intricate evolution of circumstances that sent me and
Jean to Key West, where we stayed for six years. That journey
began in Maine almost twenty years before, when our oldest children were still in junior high school. Our place in Maine, primarily
because it was true countryside and also because Jean made every
visitor feel so welcome, became a popular after-school gathering
spot for the boys' classmates. There was plenty of room for them
to hang out, lots of food and drink in the refrigerator, and a barn
loft where privacy was assured.

A few years later, one of those visitors began riding the real-
estate boom of the late 1970s and '80s. Before any of his classmates
graduated from college, he had already been certified a million-
aire by business-news reporters. As he moved on to become a
multimillionaire (in the newspapers, at least), he extended his
range from Portland, Maine, to Boston and from there to Key
West, where he bought that small, southernmost island's largest
single chunk of developable real estate: about fifty-five acres on
the waterfront.

In the meantime, I had cofounded and helped build the
Maine Times into a successful, statewide weekly journal of opinion,
a job that took most of my time for some ten years. After that, once
I knew the paper was firmly established, I began to get restless and

moved on to combine other pursuits with my diminishing responsibilities at *Maine Times*. In a few years, my work there effectively ended, even though I continued to contribute a column. But even that stopped when the publisher, my partner, sold the paper, a move that effectively blurred much of my Maine identity.

Which was precisely when our young friend made his startling purchase in Key West. The same day I read the story in *The New York Times*, I called him and asked for a job, any job, that would allow us to live in Key West, a place that I knew was surrounded by the finest saltwater game fishing in the world; and that's no exaggeration.

After more than sixty years in the northeast, almost half of that in Maine, a move to Key West is a radical transition indeed. There are seasons there, yes, but they are each variations on what New Englanders call summer. And what we know as winter up here does not even begin to exist on the island. Indeed, Key West winters are more benign than many Maine summers.

Which, for me, was too exotic to be borne with equanimity. I went off the deep end in Key West, reveling each day in the sheer sensuality of that soft, salty warmth, the tender air, and the great sheaves of sunlight that piled so palpably onto that two-by-three-mile piece of land each day. As I biked the fragrant streets I could feel the sun's weight on my shoulders, and I welcomed it as gift I had never expected. I could hardly sleep through the velvet nights, and each day I yearned to be on the emerald and azure waters that stretched to every horizon.

And while that yearning spurred me to all sorts of successful machinations that could put me in a small boat, there were still many days when the piper had to be paid, when I had to work at this job or that simply to survive. But even on those days, I would never let go of the surrounding seas. Always I would be looking toward the water, or better yet, peering down into it if I chanced to be biking across a bridge or alongside one of the island's many inlets, lagoons, harbors, or salt ponds.

And when I could do none of that, there were always the water birds that made the city of Key West yet another rookery or feeding ground or merely a bit of land where they could rest. And of these birds, none was more exotic, more subtropical, more indigenous to that salty, sultry stretch of citified coral than the white ibis. Because, like many Key West residents, it is freely given to inexplicable eccentricities.

But it is the bird's beauty in flight that first touched me, as it has surely touched millions of others who know it for the first time. This is a fairly large bird, with the long neck and legs common to most waterbirds. Its wings in flight always appear to be slightly cupped. That's how they looked when I saw my first ibis flock above me, in a kind of stately formation. There were perhaps a dozen birds, and they caught the rising sun in those cupped wings, giving the flight an ethereal rose-pink hue that spilled over the brilliant white breasts and then off the jet-black wing tips. Like so much of life in Key West, the flight was unhurried, graceful, and, above all, exotic. These were, for me, the essential tropical birds of legend, an image you might see in your dreams of mangrove hummocks, the southern Caribbean, islands that float on the horizon of your fantasies.

And if that had been my only image of the white ibis, it would still have stayed with me for all of my years. But because we lived and worked in a Key West building that boasted one of the city's largest lawns, I was to meet the bird many more times. Key West is a settlement of relatively many human beings on a definitely small island, and as a result the vast majority of its homes are hard by each other. Raise your window shade in the morning and you are likely to look directly into the eyes of your neighbor as he raises his.

Not so at our place. A definite anomaly, the building we called home sat solo in the center of a Key West city block, and all around it was lawn. This, I think, was the reason the place attracted so many birds, including, quite frequently, the white ibis, a shy waterbird not generally known to pay calls on city dwellers.

Like the one that took its place on the hood of the family car for at least a week. We parked the car in the shade of a palm tree alongside the driveway, and one early morning when I opened the front door, the ibis was simply there. And there it would stay like some giant ornament. If the car had to be used, the bird would shift its perch to a fence post, quite reluctant to leave. Every now and then it darted to the lawn, plucked a small morsel from the grass with a lightning stab of that impressive, bright-red decurved bill, and then repaired to its post or to the hood of our car for repose and digestion.

When I inquired at the Keys Audubon Society about what might account for such unusual behavior, I learned that wading birds like the ibis sometimes leave their accustomed haunts when extreme high tides make feeding all but impossible. Sure enough, I checked the tide tables and was informed that the year's highest tides were currently in process. This bit of lunar information provided a better explanation for the bird's behavior than any of the reasons I had conjured, including one based on reincarnation and the ancient Egyptians' belief that their god Thoth would take the form of an ibis on his occasional visits to earth.

The hood sitter was not our only ibis visitor. After one autumnal storm, two immature ibis, adolescents in their mixed brown and white plumage, took over the lawn for several days. From the front porch where I sat, I could watch them strutting on those long, pink legs, then stopping as they poked their pink bills with machine-gun speed into the grass roots, over and over, until I wondered what protein delicacy they were finding in such abundance.

The pair were gawky birds that blessed me with a benefit they could not have known. For as they went about their business of survival, two-legged creatures of somewhat lesser intelligence buzzed by on motor scooters, tooting tinny horns, shouting, and tossing half-empty beer cans on our curb. Yet there were the ibis through it all to reassure me that life is charged with the wild and the beautiful, as well as the thoughtless and the ugly.

All I needed to do was to take wing like the ibis and glide to the silent mangroves just offshore, and there the beauty would be.

BROWN PELICAN
(*Pelecanus occidentalis*)

Discharged from the Army Air Corps in October 1945, I had to wait until the start of new term in February to return to Yale for another try at a college education. As you might surmise, the few months that intervened were fairly sodden. At twenty-three, I considered myself indestructible, especially after surviving all those combat missions in a B-17. With money in the bank (deposits taken from my flight pay each month) and time to kill, I spent most of my nights standing at Manhattan bars, always hopeful that I would meet a mature woman with an apartment.

In those days, LaRue was my most favored drinking venue. A well-mannered nightclub on east 58th Street between Park and Madison, LaRue was home to Meyer Davis and his orchestra, and to a great many sons and daughters of the city's socially correct WASP families. Which meant that almost all the young men and women I chatted with at the bar were people I had already met. In fact, I'd known most of them for years. We'd gone to the same dancing classes and the same coming-out parties. Even after being shot at in the skies over Europe, I wasn't brave enough to visit Harlem, the West Side, or even Third Avenue.

All too aware of my shortcomings, I kept promising myself I would kick the LaRue habit, break the conventions of an upper middle-class upbringing, and find true adventure beyond the invisible boundaries of the Upper East Side. At that point in my life, "adventure" meant something like meeting Brett just as she stepped out of the pages of Hemingway's *The Sun Also Rises.*

So it was with that sort of vision pulsing in my alcoholic dreams that I responded immediately to Bo's suggestion that we hit the road for Florida. Bo's given name was Beaux, bestowed by his Paris-smitten parents shortly after they returned to Park Avenue from their Paris honeymoon. Weary of explanations by the time he was in his twenties, Bo made certain everyone knew how to spell his name. A fighter pilot with the 15th Air Force in Italy, he was even more dashing than I but equally fed up with standing at the LaRue bar six or seven nights a week.

And it was cold that night he came up with Florida. A raw wind blew hard through 58th Street, freezing, harsh, and bitter from the northeast. We were on our way by 2:30 that morning. I had sprung the family station wagon from its garage on 63rd Street; I had permission to drive it, but not to Florida. What the hell, we figured, we'd be too long gone before my father, the Plymouth's owner of record, could do very much.

I drove through the Holland Tunnel, on through New Jersey, Pennsylvania, and Maryland, where the sun rose on nearly deserted highways. Then came breakfast (we were still high on adrenaline), and Bo took the wheel while I tried to sleep, stretched out in the station wagon's copious rear. We finally stopped in Georgia, spent the night in a rundown motor-court cabin, and, late the following day, rolled into Miami Beach, where we both slept in the wagon.

The Bath & Tennis Club was the only place in town either one of us had heard of, so we drove by. I have no idea why. Perhaps we thought a WASP fairy godmother would wave as we passed, endow us with a membership, and offer us a beachfront room. No such luck, but we did spot a "Help Wanted" sign at the hotel next door. Close enough.

That soon after the war, Miami Beach hotels were still straining to reopen to the public. Most of them had been taken over by the military, and there was a great deal to be done to restore their civilian amenities. Which is how Bo and I found ourselves at work that very day, moving refrigerators into the guest suites. From there I went on to become an elevator operator and the hotel's lifeguard, which will give you some idea of how difficult it was to get good help.

Within three days Bo had cracked up the station wagon and vanished, on his way back to LaRue, I supposed. There was no way I was going to turn up at home with a station wagon minus a bumper and front fender. So there I stayed, quite alone, living on guava-jelly sandwiches, saving money for car repairs.

But those long hours on the beach were splendid. Often I could see fish flashing silver in the curl of a wave, and each day the brown pelicans glided by in their single-file formations, flying with such stunning and effortless grace that my heart beat faster. For those moments I forgot my silly job, the crumpled fender, and my father's increasing telephone calls demanding the return of his automobile.

Often the pelicans would discover the same fish I saw there in the waves. Then those graceful birds would dive, and what a show that was. They would set their broad wings, dip out of their single-file flight, fold those wings far back, flip over almost upside-down, and stiffen and straighten their entire neck and body so they became a kind of great, feathered weapon, a spear hurled powerfully at the sea's surface.

Without hesitation, those pelicans would power-dive into the waves. The impact always amazed me. Great gouts of white water would splash high in the soft air, then there would be a moment, hardly a split-second, of stillness before the pelican surfaced, almost always with a fish in that long, exotic, pouched bill. Throwing back and tilting its head, the big bird would drain away the sea water, and then, with visible gulps, swallow the fish whole, and quickly, too.

Of all the many images I brought back with me when, at last, I was able to repair the Plymouth, none stayed as bright as those flights and dives of the brown pelican. I see them still, and it was that bird's incredible, effortless flight, its mastery of the air and sea that stuck so vividly with me through so many years. Until—at long last—it helped pull me back to south Florida, where I could once again see pelicans fishing somewhere besides in my memories.

As it turns out, those memories might well have been all I had left. Shortly after I drove home alone (and, yes, went back to college) the war's chemical by-products almost exterminated the brown pelican. The widespread use of DDT and other "hard" chlorinated hydrocarbon pesticides in the agrarian deep South took a harsh and sudden toll on this bird, which feeds near the top of the food chain. By 1960, entire brown pelican populations had simply vanished from many Gulf barrier island rookeries. But gradually, as the use of the toxic pesticides began to be controlled, or prohibited completely, the brown pelican made a remarkable comeback.

It was a drama I missed. I didn't return to Florida until more than forty years after those travels with Bo. During those decades, the brown pelican all but disappeared, was declared an endangered species, and then recovered. By the time I got to Key West in 1986, some people claimed that there were too many pelicans, that they were pests, bothering anglers, crapping on boats, and sometimes pecking tourists with their bills when they wanted a handout of french fries.

I had many face-to-face encounters with pelicans, most of them while I was aboard my beat-up boat, out there fishing the channels and flats. Often while we nibbled on a luncheon sandwich, a pelican would glide in, land, and paddle up to the boat hoping for a handout. That was the problem: the big birds were fed by so many tourists, they began to believe everyone on the water owed them a tidbit. Many an angler on the hook-and-line party boats found himself fast to a pelican that had tried to swallow a baited hook. Which led to some confusion as the mate tried to free the frightened, thrashing bird. Panicked pelicans seen that closely are not the graceful creatures that charm us so on the wing.

I found that out one afternoon as I was painting my boat, just some touch-ups near the bow. I didn't need to take her out of the water. I was lying there on deck, painting prone, when a juvenile pelican paddled up and grabbed the paint brush in its bill. I yelled, grabbed it back, and slapped the bird's bill with the brush, leaving a smear of white paint about midway along that beak. I was angry at being startled, and the pelican was chagrined at its new nose job. It never tried for the brush again, but I saw it around the harbor for months. That was one bird that stood out from the pelican crowd.

The pelicans that live and fish at the Marquesas, that circular collection of wild keys twenty-five miles west of Key West, are not the sort who look for handouts. They are definitely wild birds and keep clear of anglers and their boats. I've made the trip many times in flats skiffs piloted by some of the best tarpon guides on the planet, and one of their favorite fishing spots is on the shoals that curve off to the southeast at the entrance to Mooney Harbor. It is a place where sandy shallows lie next to deep channels, and often tarpon giants swim silently from dark water and appear there on the pale sand like ancient totems, gleaming silver as they glide suddenly into your consciousness. So many times their awesome presence has set me trembling, unable to cast properly, unable to think or speak or move. I can only watch the great fish vanish in the depths.

Then I begin another search, scanning the seas for any signs of a tarpon like the one that just swam by. It's a kind of game the big fish almost always win. As I look here and there, I pay special attention to a point about a half-mile off to the southwest. Brown pelicans are always fishing there. The splashes they make when they dive (it's the impact that stuns the fish) rise like white geysers against the distant western horizon. It's a continuous spectacle, a wondrously wild, zesty drama played every day, a kind of diving dance the pelicans perform for anyone lucky enough to see it.

I count myself incredibly fortunate to have seen it many times. I was there applauding just this year, fifty years almost to the day since I first watched those Miami Beach pelicans diving for those silver fish in those luminous seas. It was this remembered image that brought me back decades later to some of the finest days of my life. For which, in so many ways, I have the brown pelican to thank.

MAGNIFICENT FRIGATE BIRD
(*Fregeta magnificens*)

It's reassuring to know that whoever named this bird was suffi-
ciently impressed to label it "magnificent." But then, I have
thought so many birds magnificent. Indeed, most of nature
strikes me this way.

Still, I can understand how anyone might be struck by the sight
of a frigate bird on the wing. Part of the impact has to be the location, for these black, dramatic birds are strictly subtropical and
coastal. With the exception of those that get blown off course by a
hurricane, they never leave the waters of the Caribbean and the Atlantic coast of south Florida. To get to know them, you must spend
time in those southernmost places where the air is soft with its
soaking by the salt sea, a sea you can breathe.

Which is one reason why this bird is such a symbol of the exotic: you meet it in such exotic places. But you would remember it
even if you saw it gliding above a supermarket parking lot. No
other bird has a greater wingspan in relation to its weight. Few have
the forked tail, few are as large, and very few have such a long
hooked bill and are so black against such a high sky.

It is often the frigate bird I see in my dreams when those
dreams are of my days on the water off Key West. Go north of that
beleaguered island a few miles along Northwest Channel until you

reach Cottrell Key, and you voyage from one world to another. While cruise-ship passengers crowd Duval Street's tacky shops, Cottrell's wildness is pure, untainted by any evidence of human-kind except what arrives there by small boat and will leave the way it came.

Because they can lay claim to this key's mangroves and button-wood trees, the frigate birds are there. If you arrive at dawn and pole your skiff silently, you can get close enough to see them perched in the trees; dark ovals against a luminous eastern hori-zon, they have the graceful curves and proportions of a Chinese vase. But slide a few feet closer above the pale shoals and the frigate birds will begin to stir. Some take flight, and their assumption of air beneath those long wings angled back from their center is a memorable moment, magnificent indeed.

For these birds are designed for flight, not perching; for glid-ing, not walking, running, or scratching the ground like wild turkeys. The air's upper reaches are where the frigate bird lives most of its life, soaring, riding the thermals like a skier on invisi-ble, airy slopes, finding hills in the sky, dipping along the rim of a great cumulus, then soaring suddenly higher on a windward thrust those of us watching from below will never feel, see, or compre-hend. We know it exists only because it has been defined by the flight of a magnificent frigate bird.

Unforgettable. Always in my dreams. Always.

Which is a great gift for any creature to give. But there is more. West of Cottrell, perhaps twenty-five miles, are the Marquesas, where those wild brown pelicans dive. And frigate birds nest. Here is perhaps the largest concentration of these mysterious seabirds in the nation, here in the most remote, southernmost territory the continental United States can claim. Here there are young frigate birds, just one to each nest, thrashing naked from the egg and then acquiring frowzy, dark body feathers and white heads and necks. Their mothers have solid white breasts, and during the courting season, males develop a surprisingly vivid crimson throat pouch, which they inflate to indicate to the ladies that the time for serious courtship has arrived.

There is a kind of uncomfortable intimacy to these encounters with frigate birds at home. The limbs of the trees in their rookery are bleached pale with accumulated guano, and the birds themselves—some of them too juvenile to take wing—are rather clumsy, flapping those great wings to hold their balance on their tiny, almost vestigial feet. These are birds fashioned first and foremost for flight; all else is secondary, even the nursery.

Alone in my small boat one afternoon, fishing for yellowtail snapper I had promised Jean I would bring back for dinner, I watched a frigate bird wheel overhead. The wind was stiff from the southeast and the surface of Northwest Channel was lumpy. A strong ebb tide challenged the wind, and standing waves hissed, tossing their whitecaps at my broad-sided boat. Too rough to fish here, I told myself. Time to hang it up and head home.

But there was that frigate bird, diving from the scudding sky, dipping bits of edible flotsam of some sort from the choppy sea, always with a swift grace and remarkable mastery of that turbulent air. Fascinated by the display, I watched for a long spell, knowing I would likely never see such a sight again. And when I did start the outboard and begin the slow voyage home, beating into the seas most of the way, that frigate bird followed me. There was, for much of that trip, a kind of communion between me and the bird. I personalized its presence, told myself we had established a rare sort of interplay, aware as we had to be of each other's presence, out there alone together on that choppy sea.

At the harbor entrance, that magnificent seabird wheeled, caught a surging updraft toward the heavens, and on motionless wings, rode the wind to freedoms we can never know. I was sad to see it go but grateful for our meeting.

Marsh Hawk

(*Circus cyaneus*)

This is one of several birds whose names have been officially changed during the span of my years. As a boy and young man, I often saw these raptors flying above the cattails that grew so profusely along the Georgica Pond waterfront at our house in East Hampton. In the spring, sitting in the dining room with its large west-facing window overlooking the pond, I would watch for the first marsh hawks of the season. Their return, like the osprey's, was yet another verification of winter's end, longer days ahead, and the coming of summer: my boyhood's happiest time of the year.

Now this hawk is called the northern harrier. Like so many official name changes, this one was made for reasons I've never known. I suppose it is more accurate: harriers are named for their harrying tendencies, and to harry means to plunder and ravage. These, however, are not the images that occur to me whenever I see a marsh hawk. The traits I associate with this impressive bird are a kind of wild grace and an embodiment of freedom. That was a state of being I sorely envied as a boy who had to spend most of his days and nights at boarding schools, where freedom was so strictly measured in such minute amounts that it was all but forbidden.

As a constant rebel against such oppressive prohibitions, I tended to acquire punishments that just about wiped even minuscule freedoms out of my life. So when our spring vacations allowed us to escape school for a week or ten days, the time spent with my

grandparents at that place on the pond was almost more of a release than my emotions could handle. For the first day or two my heart raced, I slept just a few restless hours, and before the sun rose I was dressed and walking the pond's edges or crossing the dunes to the ocean, where I was the only visible human being for all the windswept miles I could see.

My grandfather was a slim, slight man. Always dapper, with a well groomed gray mustache, he couldn't have weighed more than 125 pounds, if that. But he loved to eat, in the best sense of dining. With no servants in the house during those March and April visits, he did the cooking and made certain that he put three elegant meals on the table each day, although most days there were just the two of us. My grandmother took many of her meals on a tray in her rooms at the far end of the house.

Luncheon almost always included sandwiches, most of them made on rich, dark pumpernickel, often with tasty cheese, excellent ham, or perhaps roast beef with horseradish, or smoked salmon and cream cheese—classics all. My grandfather was not given to experimental dishes or diet foods. Most often, he'd bake a pie for dessert; if it was an apple pie, more cheese would be served, this time a crumbly cheddar. As you might imagine, after months of boarding school fare soggy off the steam table, the food alone on those precious holidays was cause for ecstasy.

But there were always more delights. My grandfather would never rush a meal; for him, each one was an experience. So we never rose from those lunches in less than an hour.

My seat at the table faced the large window; I could scan the cattails and the pond as I ate and talked, for my grandfather was also a lively conversationalist and knew how to keep an eleven year old engaged and interested. But no matter how dramatic the stories he told, I seldom took my eyes off the world beyond that window.

It was there the ospreys and the red-wings first flew into my ken, and it was there, although not so frequently, the marsh hawk came gliding, swerving, and dipping above the cattails, on the hunt. There is an unmistakable posture to the flight of these predators. At times, it seems almost clumsy: somewhere between a hover and a stall, a dip or an out-of-control dive. With a distinct white patch at the base of their tail and large wings often stretched horizontally, marsh hawks are not easily confused with any other hawk. Pale, blue-gray plumage makes the males more handsome, in my opinion. But it is the dusky-brown female I see most often, leading me to believe that she is the hardest-working provider of the family.

Because it loves the wetlands for which it was so aptly (and formerly) named, the marsh hawk has lived in the same places I have always favored above all others: places near the water. Several decades after those Georgica years, our home in Pennellville here in Maine looked out over rolling fields, marshes, and ponds that dropped off into Middle Bay a half-mile beyond. Every spring, a marsh hawk would lay claim to those lands as its hunting grounds; and once again I could look out the window from our kitchen table and watch it tilting, dipping, and gliding so buoyantly on the wind.

I have been told that there is a purpose to this apparently erratic flight. Swooping as it so often does, this hawk first flushes its quarry from cover, then darts down and grabs the field mouse, frog, rat, or rabbit in its talons and often eats it on the spot. I never saw that happen in Pennellville, but I did witness it through our current home's front windows, which also look out across a rolling field, this one less than a half-mile from the marshes of the Androscoggin River.

Here, too, we are in the marsh hawk's company. This past spring—a cold and wet one—I watched a marsh hawk on her endless hunt almost every day. How, I wondered, could she survive? How could she feed her chicks? These hawks generally have four or five to raise; sometimes as many as nine. Yet there were so many times I watched that marsh hawk when she did nothing but glide and hover on that apparently endless patrol. Then, amid the patches of an April snow, I saw her stoop, flap those long wings, and plop to the ground, almost clumsily, as if she had lost her air speed. There she stayed for ten minutes or so, her head darting down and pulling back as she dissembled her prey into bite-size servings.

At last, I told myself, she has found food. But what of those chicks? I gave up worrying, of course. There was surely nothing I could do to alter the circumstances of that hawk's quest to feed her family. Yet she stayed a stubborn presence until June, out there every day, good weather and foul, and it was surely foul more than fair.

What an awesome responsibility, I thought, to awake every morning knowing your offspring's survival depends on your skills and persistence as a hunter. Surely none of us nor our children could deal with such a challenge. No doubt about it: we have an easier life than a marsh hawk mother. I tell myself that whenever I see her now and again as she patrols her territory.

In a few weeks she and her family will be leaving on their long migration, following the sun and their prey to South American marshes. I wonder if there are boys there who await this hawk's arrival as intently as I did those many years ago and as I still am able to do because we are fortunate enough to live by the wetlands and rolling fields these splendid harriers find so much to their liking.

RING-NECKED
PHEASANT
(Phasianus colchicus)

According to most sources, the ring-necked pheasant was first introduced to the United States in 1880 by Judge O. N. Denny, the U.S. Consul at Shanghai, who shipped a number of the birds to his farm near Pattersons Butte in Oregon. It is also said that two years later an open hunting season on the birds was declared and some 50,000 ringnecks were shot the first day.

Like so many gunners, those nineteenth-century Oregonians surely exaggerated their shooting skills. However, with a bird as easy to kill as the ringneck, they probably didn't stretch the truth by too many thousands.

I now regret shooting the large numbers of pheasant that I have killed during my twentieth-century years as a boy and young man. For as I have learned more about this odd bird I have come to sympathize with its plight. Few natural creatures have been as crassly manipulated by self-serving men as the ringneck.

The manipulation that began with Judge Denny continues to this day. After more than a century, the ringneck is still being "introduced" to new corners of the nation, where it is hoped the flocks will survive and multiply so they can become yet another "game" bird. This concept of creating more and more targets for wing shooters is what creates jobs for more and more people on state wildlife agency payrolls. And it is most often the ringneck that pays with its life.

Perhaps, ironically, I feel for this creature because I have always considered it a dumb bird with a pea brain quite unfit for survival in the wild. And the chief reason for my low opinion of a ringneck's IQ is that I was able to kill so many of them.

I started young. I was fifteen when I looked out a window of that house on Georgica and saw a cock pheasant strolling across our lawn. He was a dramatic, large bird and, as I also knew, was supposed to be more delicious out of the oven than the finest roasted chicken. I took my grandfather's twist-steel, hammerlock, 10-gauge double and walked after the pheasant, hoping it would fly so I could shoot at it. My unwillingness to kill a bird on the ground, even in those teenage days, can be taken as a tribute to a proper WASP upbringing. It just wasn't done.

Pheasants are fast walkers and faster runners. This bird picked up the pace considerably as it headed for the bayberries at the far west end of the property. I followed and the pheasant vanished in the brushy cover. But there was only a small patch between the road and the pond. Starting from the road and walking noisily toward the water, I forced the pheasant to run out of hiding space. When it flushed and flew noisily almost straight up, I dropped it cleanly with one shot. I'd broken several laws in the process, but as I held that dramatically feathered pheasant high in my hand, I was proud beyond measure. And equally proud when the bird was served at dinner the next evening.

Ringnecks, I learned later, had been raised and released on Long Island's East End for years. I never fully understood the rationale. Inside East Hampton Village limits—which included our house on Georgica—it was illegal to fire any sort of gun. (That was one of the laws I'd violated.) Thus any pheasant that wandered across the village boundaries found itself in a kind of sanctuary. I'm certain those dimwitted, overbred birds never knew the extent of their legal protection, but they did nest and raise their young with no interference from hunters. Feral house cats—and there were many of those in the Hamptons—weasels, foxes, and hawks must have found pheasant chicks easy pickings, but even so, the birds multiplied prodigiously.

Their voices became part of my summer awakenings. Like their distant relations in the poultry family, cock pheasants crow when the sun rises and for quite a while afterwards. Theirs is a most distinctive, metallic call, a kind of *honk, honk,* except there is, as far as I know, no phonetic combination that can realize the unique brassiness of the voice. It's a sound quite unlike any other in nature, instantly recognizable, and forceful enough to carry long distances, especially on the still, damp air of a summertime early morning.

Lying in my bed listening, I visualized the strutting cock bird, just like the one I had shot. And sometimes I considered getting up and dressed, taking the shotgun, and killing another. But I never did; bed felt too blissful, and I knew that the odds were I'd never flush the bird anyway.

I also probably suspected, even then, that there would be many more, easier opportunities to kill pheasants. And I was right. In my first year as a commercial fisherman (a remarkably unsuccessful one), I was a guest of Jim Reutershan in his Newton Lane home. I had a small room in his attic, and we were partners in our efforts to make a living "on the water." Jim had been a P-40 fighter pilot during the war. Both of us were considered rather dashing young men by folks who didn't know us too well. And both of us had reputations as marksmen, especially as wing shots.

Which was why we were invited to take part in pheasant shoots, a kind of recreational activity for gunners. Outfits that raised pheasants, just as chickens are raised in pens, organized these shoots. There was nothing complex about the events: some twelve or fifteen gunners took their places about a gunshot apart in a circle at the bottom of a small hill. At the top, a man was stationed in the midst of small crates that held captive pheasants. One by one they would be taken out and tossed high in the air. Squawking and disoriented, they would fly in the first direction that entered their heads; wherever it was, it took them within range of a shooter. Because the shoot cost less if more pheasants were killed (they could be sold by the farm) it benefited the organizers to invite the best wing shots. Which is how Jim and I got there. Between us, we killed fifty-two ringnecks one morning. We missed three birds.

Given that sort of wretched excess, you might think I'd had my fill of pheasant shooting. But I persisted for several more years, including an unauthorized landing on Gardiners Island with Sonny Wainwright in his Cessna. With the prop still turning, we jumped from the plane, kicked up several pheasant from the cover alongside the runway, killed two, tossed them in the cockpit, and took off before Charley Raynor could get there in his pickup. Given Charlie's reputation as a hard-nosed gamekeeper, we were mightily relieved to be off the ground.

Looking back, I realize how often the ringneck played a role in my youthful years. In training as a B-17 crew member in Sioux Falls, South Dakota, I knocked over an officer one night as I ran, trying to get to the mess hall before the rush. No malice was intended; the guy was in my way in the dark. Nevertheless, I was court-martialed and sentenced to two weeks on the rock pile. As prisoners, we were marched off the base each day to a field full of rocks, which we were ordered to break into small bits with our sledgehammers. The cornfields around us were full of ringnecks, and it was the sound of their calling and the sight of them strutting that made those days pass so much more easily.

And after I'd flown some twenty missions with the 452nd Bomb Group, our crew was given a rest. Sent to some British peer's estate that had been taken over by the Red Cross, we had little or nothing to do each day except wander the grounds or play card games indoors. I wandered, and wherever I walked, it seemed, I flushed pheasants. Lord Whoever must have planned many a shoot for his friends, I thought, delighted to see this bird that had been such a part of my less hazardous past. Hearing the cocks honk there in the early morning, I could forget being shot at for awhile and be back in my boyhood bed, safe from the risks of combat.

Which was the beginning of a changed relationship with the ringneck, although the change was slow in coming. As the years passed, I found myself less and less inclined to even think about killing one more ringneck, although during the years we lived on an old farm outside Dayton, Ohio, there were plenty of pheasants on the property. Even in Maine, the ringneck followed me. On the state's southern coast, where the winters are milder (strictly a comparative term), various rod-and-gun clubs have never quit trying to establish a pheasant population, even though history has all but proved that not enough birds will make it through the winter to sustain a renewal. Still, the pheasants are released each September, shot at, and then left to survive the winter as best they can. It is "game management" at its worst but is also the logical extension of the sort of thinking that inspired Judge Denny to send a few hundred Chinese "chickens" from Shanghai to Oregon.

This undeniably handsome, but quite witless, bird has been little more than a target ever since. So imagine my joy when I awakened one raw Maine morning last March, looked out the bedroom window, and saw a robust, bright, long-tailed ringneck cock strutting across our lawn as if he owned the place.

"You made it, you lucky bastard," I yelled at him through the glass. "You made it. Have a great summer. And, I hope, a long and happy life."

I was, I know, trying to atone for my pheasant sins. But I was truly happy to see that one impressive bird, and on our lawn. Almost sixty years after I'd seen my first ringneck on another lawn of ours, I felt the birds and I had realized the basis for a much more humane and sustaining relationship.

WHIMBREL
(*Numenius phaeopus*)

❧

When I shot and killed the only whimbrel I have seen in all my years, it was called the Hudsonian curlew, one of the family of shorebirds that once darkened the skies of this nation's Atlantic Coast.

I was probably fourteen when I did the deed. That was the summer I discovered our maternal grandfather's shotgun in a garret closet of our place on Georgica. I first fired it from a distance, with a string tied to one of the two triggers and the double-barreled gun fastened to a wooden crate. I had cut two good-sized notches in each end of the box so the ten-gauge could rest there fairly steadily. I pulled back both hammers but ran the string from just one trigger. I wanted to see if the firing of one shell would jar the other hammer loose. The impact of both barrels, I surmised, might be enough to rupture the old gun.

I put the box and the gun on the beach, about halfway between the ocean and the dunes. The string was long enough to let me lie prone at the edge of the dunes. When I yanked, the gun fired with an awesome roar, pellets ripped into an advancing wave, and the wooden box slammed back an inch or two. But the gun survived intact. I freed it from the box, put it to my shoulder, and with my heart pounding mightily, pulled the second trigger.

I felt the jolt the full length of my body, and most sharply at the bony hollow between my shoulder and my collarbone; with its

straight stock, that ten-gauge had a punishing kick. But I could take it, I told myself, my heart still thumping at the thought that I was now in possession of a real man's gun. It was a heady moment.

Within a few days, I had become a hunter, even though the legal hunting season was weeks away, I was still too young to even apply for a hunting license and I had no idea which birds—if any—could be shot at. The fact that I had a shotgun I could call my own was the only reason I needed to start killing.

Wandering the dunes near the Georgica Gut, I searched for the mourning doves I had often seen there. They did not cooperate, but as I looked carefully over the crest of a dune on the Georgica side of that sand spit between the ocean and the pond, I saw a solitary, large, brown bird at the water's edge, dipping its long bill into the shallows.

I stood and aimed the shotgun at the bird. It refused to fly. Indeed, it took little notice of my presence, even though I wasn't more than forty feet away. Chagrined, I eased down the side of the dune until I reached the narrow Georgica beach. Even then, the bird would not take wing, although it did take a few long, graceful steps, lifting its spindly legs with a fine aplomb as if to prove that it would remain undisturbed by any intruder.

Holding the gun with one hand, I picked up a surf clam shell from the sand and skimmed it at the bird. That got it airborne, although not with any urgency. It merely flapped its surprisingly long wings a time or two and began a glide back toward the beach. It was still gliding when I shot it.

When I picked it up, warm and limp in my hands, I realized it was a bird I had never before seen. Larger than any shorebird in my experience, it had a long bill that curved down, as if it had been gently bent. Even though in those years I knew very little, I knew this was not an everyday visitor to the Georgica shores.

I also knew anyone with two eyes could have killed it with a shotgun. My conquest—and the notion that that's what it was vanished quickly—had required no skill. If I'd wanted to and had been any good at all, I could have thrown a stone at the bird and killed it.

But there it was, bloody and warm in my hands. Increasing

waves of shame and guilt were fast eroding any pride I had taken in my hunting prowess. Soon my shame became so insistent and my fear of being found out so alarming that I found a piece of driftwood and used it to dig a fairly deep hole in the sand where I buried the bird I had just killed.

Weeks later, I met Doc Helmuth at the Georgica shore, less than a half-mile from where I shot the large shorebird. I described the bird, never telling him I'd killed it, just that I'd seen it on the Georgica flats.

"Almost certainly a Hudsonian curlew," he told me. "You're lucky you saw it. They're not too common here. Accidental, really. They stop by for a bite on their way from the Arctic, back to Tierra del Fuego. That's probably where your bird was headed. They're there for the southern hemisphere's summer and here for ours.

"Lovely birds. Lovely birds," he said wistfully. "I wish I'd seen it. Have to keep my eyes open. Sometimes when they stop over they stay a week or so. Not too many of them left in the world now. Shot 'em all to hell, they did, back before there were any gunning laws. Some of those shorebirds, they were just too trusting. I don't believe they ever understood they were being hunted. Why, the night hunters here on Long Island wouldn't even bother with guns. They'd shine a light on those shorebirds and step right up and wring their necks."

It's been damn close to sixty years since I killed that curlew and I can still feel it in my hands, still see what havoc I wrought with such juvenile bravado and a kind of unforgivable ignorance. But then, isn't unforgivable ignorance part of what being fourteen years old and male is all about? Not only did I kill that rare bird, but I buried it on the spot—a total waste. And then I lied about what I had done, many times.

But, as you can see, not without guilt.

I am reassured, however, by my friend Peter Matthiessen, who lives at Sagaponack, not too far from the Georgica Gut. In his splendid essay for the book *The Shorebirds of North America*, Peter writes: ". . . meeting a whimbrel one fine summer day of February in Tierra del Fuego, I wondered if I had not seen this very bird a half year earlier at home."

Those words were set down some thirty years after I killed that curlew at Georgica, which allows me the small consolation of knowing it was not the last of its kind. In 1937, give or take a few hundred whimbrels, it could well have been.

RED-BREASTED
MERGANSER
(Mergus serrator)

We—my brother Chick and I and every gunner we knew—always called them sheldrake, a name I have also seen spelled shelldrake. That might make more sense if these diving ducks ate shellfish, which they do not; they eat fish, almost exclusively, and are well equipped for it.

Older texts also refer to them as sawbills, a more easily traced name because their long, hooked, almost cylindrical bills are indeed fitted with tiny saw teeth, upper and lower. Our name, sheldrake, was loosely applied to any member of the merganser family, of which there are three: the common merganser, the red-breasted, and the hooded. This last is the smallest of the trio, and we have met only recently. A handsome, dapper waterfowl, the hooded merganser drake has an impressive, black-trimmed white crest that it wears especially well during its spring courtship. Which is when I see both male and female on the stream just behind our home here in Maine. I'm certain they are nesting somewhere close by, but they are extremely shy after their offspring are hatched, and we never see them again.

Watching these striking birds, and feeling privileged to be able to, I often think back to the days when Chick and I knew their relatives as sheldrake. It seems those were times in another life, yet I know they were not. One reason is that sheldrake have followed me through all my years, turning up wherever circumstance has taken me. Fishing for salmon on the Upsalquitch in New Brunswick, I've seen sheldrake fly past our canoe, just a foot or so above the river's bright surface, their white wing patches flashing in the sunlight.

If Jim Moores was my guide, he would swing an imaginary shotgun at the birds, pull its invisible trigger and say, "*Boom!*" making certain the ducks knew they'd just been shot down.

"They eat the parr, them damned ducks," he would say, drawing out the word parr, making it sound much closer to "pear." Parr being the young of the year of the Atlantic salmon, the fish responsible for most of Jim Moores' annual income, it was easy to understand why he resented the presence of these predators. Especially when they flew so smugly within a few feet of a guide who had not yet been able to put his angler in touch with a salmon.

Sheldrake must be used to this sort of animosity by now. Because they do dine almost exclusively on small fish, they have been blamed since the turn of the century for the decline of this or that sporting species. It used to be that wildfowlers who had utterly no use for the sheldrake as a table bird—because they taste like old fish instead of roast duck—would knock down any sheldrake that came within range and leave it where it fell. The conviction that a dead sheldrake would mean more fish for anglers everywhere was righteous justification for this casual slaughter.

But, as is so often the case, it was almost always an act of man that caused the declines, and sometimes failures, of fisheries around the planet. Recent studies by biologists who have examined the stomachs of hundreds of sheldrake "collected" for the research prove that most of the fish these ducks catch in those artfully equipped, sawtooth bills are coarse fish, so-called "trash fish" that compete with parr for the available food. By preying on the parr's competition, mergansers are doing as least as much to help the fishery as the anglers who damn all sheldrake as salmon killers.

So when I see red-breasted mergansers flying low up or down the stretch of the Androscoggin River that lies just beyond our backyard, I wonder at the changed values affecting their existence.

And I also wonder if this bird's slowly evolving transition from pariah to solid citizen has affected its numbers. If indeed it is not being so readily shot on sight, are there more sheldrake now than there were some fifty years ago, when Chick and I and our fellow duck hunters would drop one whenever it came within range?

I have the feeling that there are fewer of them. And not because hunting pressures have increased. They haven't. But breeding grounds for every wild duck have been shrinking at a fairly steady pace. If it weren't for outfits like Ducks Unlimited, which buys up and protects waterfowl nesting grounds, and the increased protection ducks continue to get from federal and state agencies, the entire roster of waterfowl species would be even shorter than it is. In other words, without being subjected to regulations, limits, and prohibitions, gunners like the one I used to be and real-estate developers who bulldoze wetlands could easily have combined to just about wipe out sheldrakes and their waterfowl brethren.

Seeing a sheldrake on the wing these days often triggers a chain reaction of remorse, guilt, and wonder at the outrageous innocence of my youthful brutality. I don't believe most Americans comprehend the blood lust of those males born fairly early in the twentieth century. We came just after the conquest of the Great Plains—the domination and near extermination of the American Indian—and long before the radical realignment of the relationship between man and nature that began with increased environmental awareness and the values typified by Earth Day.

Our heedless killing of wild creatures was even more zealous if we considered it a good deed. If, for example, we were told crows ate the eggs of songbirds—which they do—then the more crows we could shoot, the better we could feel about it. So it was with the sheldrake: "killer of young game fish." If we could drop twenty in one afternoon, we could walk away from their carcasses telling ourselves we had won a skirmish in the war to protect trout and salmon. Which not only had no basis in scientific fact, but was never the reason we killed mergansers.

We did that for fun. And we had the most fun when a late

October wind blew hard from the southeast. On one of those wet, stormy days as the open Atlantic seethed with whitecaps tumbled by the onshore gale, we sat in rain behind scrubby beach plum bushes in the curve of Gardiners Bay at Devon. There the bay turns a corner as it pokes in from the northwest and cuts sharply east toward Montauk. When the wind blows from the southeast, there is a perfect lee at the apex of that corner, which is where we set out our sheldrake decoys.

No one ever manufactured merganser decoys; they were carved from pine blocks over generations of winters by baymen who knew the duck's fondness for "stooling"—a gunner's term for any waterfowl's affection for its wooden likeness. And those drake decoys were likenesses of consummate art. Each crest rose in proud plumage from the heads of the males; every bill was painted a sheldrake red-orange; and the narrow, curved bodies were absolute replicas of the bird's intricate coloring: white wing patches; a bold, white collar around the necks of the males; a touch of cinnamon on the breast. We hauled these works of art around in a burlap potato sack, banging them against each other, chipping paint, and sometimes breaking off bills. They were sheldrake decoys, nothing more. And if we hit one or two with a load of No. 6 shot, no one cared. Some baymen we knew had a half a cellar full of sheldrake stools.

Of course, now they are worth real money. Good ones—authentic, hand-carved merganser decoys—fetch $500 and up. I haven't the slightest memory of whatever became of ours. I know they worked. We probably killed twenty or twenty-five sheldrake that stormy afternoon at the Devon bend. Years later, when I first arrived in Maine, I killed even more from a pit blind dug in the sand at the entrance to Wells Harbor. We didn't need any decoys. A southeast gale drove those sheldrake in off the ocean, one flock after another. With a thirty-five-mile-per-hour wind behind them, they had to be flying at better than sixty miles per hour. When we folded one, it would hit the water like a skipped stone, bouncing five or six times before it stayed down and floated off with the incoming tide.

Fishing the flats west of Key West, standing there for hours on the bow of a skiff, I'd see three or four sheldrake fly by, those white wing patches flashing. And I'd think how stubborn and tough this fish duck must be. I see it far north in New Brunswick and far south off the Marquesas; I see it wherever I go, and it flies past as if nothing had ever happened. As if all those sheldrake we killed so thoughtlessly never mattered, never made a difference.

They did to me. And always will.

BELTED KINGFISHER
(*Ceryle alcyon*)

❧

I
f I ever get to the Malay Archipelago, I'll look for all the other members of the kingfisher family that live and fish there. According to certified ornithologists, there are at least eighty species (some say more) scattered around the globe, with most of them favoring the exotic climate of the Pacific's Asian shores. I've been a few places—Russia, most of Europe, North Africa, Iceland, the Caribbean—but never to the far Pacific. So the belted kingfisher, being the only member of its family that visits the eastern half of these United States, is the only kingfisher I know.

It's a bird quite unto itself, distinctive and unmistakable. And it's a splendid angler. That combination of individuality and fishing skills are traits I like to think I also possess. The belted kingfisher, as its name implies, is, like me, a snappy dresser, always trim, decked out in blue-grays, russets, and some interesting accessories like a touch of white on its shoulders and, interestingly, barred tail feathers. It's an altogether dapper bird, with an imposing head and a true dagger of a black bill that's designed for just one occupation: catching and killing fish.

But the kingfisher is also, and rather unexpectedly, a world-class chatterer. Suppose you are rowing a small boat, or paddling a canoe, and you round a point and cruise up into a cove. If the waters are clear and there are trees along the shore, the chances are good that you'll meet a kingfisher. It will be perched on a high branch, one that allows an unobstructed view of the waters below, and—not coincidentally—a complete scan of the approaches to its perch. For of all the scores of birds that are constantly on the alert, few are more sensitive to intrusion than the kingfisher.

As soon as it spots you and your watercraft heading even remotely in its direction, the kingfisher takes flight. And as it does, it sounds a chattering alarm quite unlike the voice of any other bird. The sound is brassy, dissonant, and constant, like a needle stuck on an especially old, raspy, seventy-eight-r.p.m. record at the one spot where the cornet player hit an especially sour note. It's an angry sound; you know the kingfisher is irritated at your invasion of its space, the territory it had staked out for its next meal.

Chattering, it takes wing, flying erratically, as kingfishers do, dipping down on one flap of its wings, up on another. The bird abandons its position, but it doesn't go far. Kingfishers are territorialists. They take a kind of possession of their fishing grounds, defending them against intruders. To leave the area entirely would signify a surrender, and that's not at all what is on the kingfisher's mind. So it flies a couple of hundred feet to another perch and watches. If you insist on following, it moves on until, if you have forced the bird to the boundaries of its fiefdom, it flies back past you to its farthest property line. If you want, you can return there and start the entire process over again.

Only a determined kingfisher harasser would do such a thing, and there are few of those. Indeed, most folks never see this wary and solitary bird. It is the companion of those who share its drive to fish. Compulsive anglers, like me, who would think nothing of fishing through an entire day and the next if circumstances permitted, are the kingfisher's most frequent companions.

Often if my fishing is slow, I watch the kingfisher do what it does best. When it spots a fish from its lookout, just as ocean-going fishermen watch for tuna from their boat's crow's nest or tower, the kingfisher takes wing. Once over its quarry, it hovers. With extremely rapid wingbeats—something like an oversize hummingbird's—the kingfisher hovers in a single, precise spot. I'm certain you would hear those wingbeats if you could get close enough.

Sometimes it seems to me it hovers for a very long time, waiting, I suppose, for that critical moment when it is sure of its quarry. Then, in a remarkable shift of its flight attitude, it folds back its wings and feet, extends that long, black beak, and plunges headlong toward the water in an all-out power dive. But in spite of this speed, the kingfisher never goes completely underwater, as I have seen osprey do. There's a violent splash, the briefest of hesitations, and—ninety-nine times out of a hundred—this master angler takes wing with a silver fish wriggling crossways in that dagger of a beak,

There are, I suppose, better ways to spend a day. But I can't think of any. Fishing and fish watching are my two favorite activities, and this is about all (besides the basic functions of living) that a kingfisher does with its time, from sunrise to sunset. It follows the fish wherever they go. When ice begins to cloak Maine's ponds, rivers, and coastal bays, the kingfisher flies south. And in the summer, when the South's heat can become punishing, this fine, talented, handsome, and independent bird wings its way back to Maine.

I don't spend a great deal of time worrying about the afterlife. I was dead for a while, or so I've been told by surgeons who should know. I was on their operating table. When I recovered, I realized being dead isn't that bad.

Nevertheless, like many folks, I toy with the concept of reincarnation. I simply can't be convinced that wasting souls is part of nature's grand plan. Natural forces each work toward a kind of immortality. Recycling and renewal are natural ways of life and death, so why would a soul be wasted?

If I don't make it back as an osprey, I'd like my soul to be recycled into a kingfisher. After all, we already have so much in common.

AMERICAN BLACK DUCK
(Anas rubripes)

❧

O n December 18, 1941, eleven days after Pearl Harbor, Chick and I had the finest black-duck shooting of our lives. It mattered little to us that the nation was at the brink of war hysteria, or that there had been reports of Japanese submarines off California. We were college freshmen on our Christmas vacation, staying with Jimmy Edwards at the cottage on his father's big place in Sag Harbor.

In our late teens, we each knew we would soon be on the Selective Service rolls. We knew we would have to go to war, but neither of us was especially concerned about the prospect. It merely added to our determination to make the absolute most of that duck-shooting trip.

Which meant concentrating on black duck. On eastern Long Island, the black duck was the king of waterfowl. Extremely wary, fast, clever, strong, and delicious (if ever one could be brought down), that one bird had become the central deity of our gunning mythology. Ever since we first lifted a shotgun to our shoulder, the black duck had been our most revered and most ardently pursued trophy.

We spared no effort to possess it. From the very tip of Montauk Point to the bogs and ponds of Shinnecock, we traveled close to a hundred miles on some days, searching for black duck. But these wise birds had learned to tell time during the hunting season. Unless

the weather was wretched—a snowstorm or raging northeaster—the great flocks of black duck that migrated the Atlantic flyway in those days would leave their bays and potholes and ponds just before sunrise. Flying a mile or so out into the open Atlantic, they would gather in vast, undulating rafts on the heaving sea. And there they would stay until after sunset, when they would return in scattered groups, whirling like moths at a flame above the sheltered waters where they would spend the night.

Although we were well aware of the black duck's clever evasive action, we spent a great deal of time and energy trying to surprise one or two from the small bogs and potholes they favored. We called it jump shooting because black ducks are members of the marsh duck family that includes the mallard and gadwall, each able to take off vertically from the smallest patch of water. The launch is so sudden and so incredibly fast that the shooter almost always fires too late, or too low. Which was what we did.

Missing a duck is always a disappointment, but it is intensely depressing after a thirty-minute crawl through dank thickets and across mucky ground. So driven was our determination, however, that we would, almost cheerfully, leave one pothole and head for another. And there were scores, for the entire reach of Long Island's sandy soil had been gouged by Ice Age glaciers that left all manner of depressions and sinks in their wake.

But our jump-shooting plans were thwarted on that December expedition. Deep cold—record-setting, below-zero cold—had swept over the island, pushed from the far north by a powerful high-pressure system that roared in on the wings of a northwest gale. Even the salt bays were frozen hard along their shores, while mush ice spread like a quilt over the normally open waters far offshore. Only the Atlantic defied the harsh freeze, but its sand beaches were rock hard and ice crystals gathered in windrows where sluggish waves broke on the beach. Jump shooting was quite impossible; every pothole had completely congealed, solid ice from top to bottom.

Someone, perhaps it was our friend Harry Steele, whose father was East Hampton's chief of police, told us about a spring-fed pond near Mecox Bay, west of Southampton. Like us, a gunner, Harry had spent much of his boyhood and young manhood hunting and fishing the place he knew so well. Which is why we listened carefully when he told us where he thought we could find the pond that never froze.

We spent that bitter, wind-tossed afternoon searching and we found it at the edge of a potato field, probably half a mile from the shore of Mecox. About the size of a one-car garage, the pond (which is a large name for that small spot of liquid) must have been fed by a very robust underground spring, for there was open water there, just a puddle of it bubbling and gurgling in a slight depression at a far corner of the snowbound potato field.

Dumping our decoys from a burlap bag, we set out six, wooden black-duck lookalikes, three in the burbling spring water and three on the ice around it. On that day, just three days short of the winter solstice, sunset would come at just after four. It was already close to three-thirty by the time we found the pond and got the decoys in place. We couldn't build a blind because there was nothing within a mile except bare and frozen fields. So we lay on our backs in what was left of the browned cattails that grew around the slough's edges. And there in the snow, we waited.

Not for long. The sun's bottom had yet to touch the crisp horizon before we saw the first flight of six or seven black ducks headed our way. Silhouetted against the orange western sky, they were the essence of wild waterfowl, their wings beating fast until they reached our field. Then their circling began. Usually, these extremely cautious birds will fly over a potential landing site at least three times, often more. If they see anything that arouses their suspicion, especially movement of any kind, however slight (even the blinking of a gunner's eye), they leave to investigate another venue.

But these blacks circled just once and then came whirling down like falling leaves, as cold air whistled through their extended primaries and they lowered their spread, orange, webbed feet. To a duck hunter, there is no sound as thrilling as that sibilant, almost musical singing of the wind through the cupped wings of a black duck about to land. It is, on its own, a pure, unique sound of the wild; it is also able to be heard only when the bird is rushing within shooting range. First heard, it sets the heart pounding, knees quaking, and adrenaline pumping.

For a moment or two, we could not believe those blacks would keep coming. After all, we had no cover to screen us, and although we stayed as still as we could, we had to believe any bird looking down would recognize us as alien to the landscape. But distressed by the biting cold, desperate for fresh water, those ducks tumbled toward us. As they spread their wings wide, braking, and hovered there for a split second above our decoys, Chick and I sat up and fired.

Two black ducks thumped to the snow and lay there.

Even as I started to get to my feet to retrieve them, Chick said, "Here comes another bunch."

And so they did, off the ocean like the first. These were even less wary. They homed straight at the water hole, made a sort of half-circle and came on in. We fired, and again ducks fell to the snow.

The shooting was almost constant after that. Our gun barrels got so hot we could feel the heat even through our wool shooter's mittens with their slots for our trigger fingers.

By sunset, when the approaching birds were dark shapes against a darkening sky, the snow around us was littered with black-duck carcasses. And still their wings whistled above us in the gathering night as hundreds more sought that winter spring.

As we got stiffly to our feet and began collecting the dusky shapes from the snow, still more ducks came in waves. Some landed among the decoys even though we were walking just a few feet away. We picked up twenty-three dead black ducks. The limit in those days was twenty, but we weren't worried about being checked by a warden. With the temperature dropping below zero for the second night, we knew every sane person would be home keeping warm.

The next morning we drove to the city with the sack of black ducks in the trunk. We gave them to our father who took them to the Union League Club where they were dressed and hung in a walk-in refrigerator. The following week, just before Christmas, he invited most of the club members to a wild duck dinner, courtesy of the Cole brothers, John and Chick.

Before the new year had gathered any momentum, Chick had volunteered for the U.S. Navy and I was on my way to an Army Air Corps training camp. We never forgot that afternoon and evening with those hundreds of black duck. It was a shoot that surpassed even our wildest duck-hunting fantasies.

I told the story many times, and no one was more taken with it than Roddy, our younger brother. Just ten years old then, he was too young for the adventure. But, oh how he wanted to go. Already an enthusiastic naturalist, he drew fine sketches of birds and animals, made many visits to the city's Natural History Museum, and talked constantly about the expeditions he planned. Animated, bright, and charged with a fine, restless energy, he was as much my companion as my brother, in spite of the eight years between us.

When I came home from three years with the Air Corps, Roddy gave me a pencil portrait of a black duck. I still have it. "To John from Pard, 1945" reads the notation in the lower right-hand corner. Pard was one of the nicknames we shared. He knew the black duck was the ultimate icon of those years when we yearned so to be outdoors, to explore the natural presences around us, to lose ourselves in the excitement and drama of places that belonged to the creatures of the wild.

Roddy knew this. Along with the black-duck portrait he gave me a scrapbook he compiled. Titled *After The War,* it was a pictorial guide to each of the places we would go, each of the wild birds, animals, and fish we would meet. Of these, the first and most important was the black duck. I still have that notebook with its carefully mounted photographs and handwritten legends.

But we never got to make any of the trips. Midway through his second year at Princeton, Roddy loaded a shotgun and took his own life. After his funeral, instead of flowers I put a black-duck wing on his grave.

I've never understood all the reasons why he did what he did, never fully recovered from the loss. A few months later while I was scalloping in Three Mile Harbor, not that far from Mecox, a lone black duck flew over my skiff, circled, and appeared to follow me as I headed back to the dock. I saw the bird again the next day. I've always believed it was a messenger sent by Roddy to say a proper farewell.

Black-duck populations continue to decline in each of its flyways, yet I still see the birds every autumn. Always they remind me of my two brothers.